becoming
FREE

CHRISTY MONSON

becoming
FREE

A WOMAN'S GUIDE TO INTERNAL STRENGTH

Copyright © 2013 by Christy Monson

All rights reserved.

Published by Familius LLC, www.familius.com

Familius books are available at special discounts for bulk purchases for sales promotions, family or corporate use. Special editions, including personalized covers, excerpts of existing books, or books with corporate logos, can be created in large quantities for special needs. For more information, contact Premium Sales at 559-876-2170 or email specialmarkets@familius.com

Library of Congress Catalog-in-Publication Data
2013943964

pISBN 978-1-938301-84-1
eISBN 978-1-938301-85-8

Printed in the United States of America

Edited by Aven Rose and Amy Stewart
Cover design by David Miles
Book design by Maggie Wickes

10 9 8 7 6 5 4 3 2 1

First Edition

Contents

Becoming Free xi

Part 1: Prescription for Work Ethic 1
    Long-Term Goals 3
    Short-Term Goals 9
    Alleviating Procrastination 16
    Being Responsible for Life Choices 23

Part 2: Approach to Self-Care 31
    The Gifts of an Imperfect Life 33
    Healing Fear 41
    Finding Personal Power 47
    Decision Making: Releasing Confusion 55
    Decision Making: Self-Trust 60
    Personal Honesty 68
    Being Sufficient 76
    Becoming Positive 82
    Allowing Imperfection in Life 87
    Releasing Depression 92

Part 3: Communication Proficiency 103
    Letting Go of Negativity in Relationships 105
    Finding Positive Thinking Patterns 112
    Listening Blocks, Listening Aids 122
    Bridling Emotionality 130
    Thinking before Speaking 138
    Control Versus Trust 145
    Self-Responsibility 152
    Positivity in Relationships 161
    Feeling Free in Relationships 170

Part 4: Practicing the Process **179**
    Keys to Success 181
    Meditation 184
    Writing Your Own Script 189
    Inner Wisdom 198
    Gratitude 200
    Creating Gifts 206
    Write, Write, Write 210
    Thought Stopping and Thought Substitution 216
    Becoming New 219
    Desensitization 224
    Laughter 228
    Communication: Listening and Reflecting 231
    Accountability Groups 237
    What Successful People Have 241
    A Higher Power 246
    Service 250
    Love 252

Conclusion **256**

Bibliography **257**

About Christy Monson **264**

I am grateful to my husband and children for their unfailing love and support. Thanks also to my critique group for helping me become a better writer: Drieniem Hatting, Lynda Scott, Patricia Bossano, and Michelle McKinnon. Deepest appreciation also goes to my editor, Aven Rose. Her expertise, good ideas, and critical feedback have enhanced the writing of this book. I am grateful for her support and guidance in arranging and assembling the manuscript.

Foreword

Free yourself from the skewed perspectives stemming from archaic childhood beliefs. These youthful misconceptions can serve as barriers in adulthood to keep love and positive energy at arm's length, denying you the quality of life you deserve.

Through concrete goal setting, understanding childhood misconceptions, journaling, and positive self-talk, past assumptions can be shed and positive energy can be yours—leading you toward peace and healthy relationships.

This book will guide you through a step-by-step process with specific assignments at the end of each chapter to help you enhance your quality of life. The techniques described were developed over the years I worked in private practice. It was exciting for me to watch each of my clients release feelings associated with youthful fallacies and juvenile trauma and acquire a new perspective about themselves.

I am grateful to each person I counseled. I learned many things from them, including what it's like to suffer, endure, and survive difficult circumstances. One never enters into a relationship without experiencing a new viewpoint.

This book contains some of my clients' stories. I present them here so that you might find a new outlook also. The names have been changed, of course, and the circumstances of each incident have been altered so that they are no longer recognizable.

The material offered in this publication is not to be used to treat, diagnose, or advise about an illness or a difficulty. If you are in need of medical assistance or expert advice for psychological, medical, legal, or financial services, please consult a specialist in the professional field required.

Introduction

Becoming Free

I sat in the warm sunshine, watching a delicate blue butterfly flit from flower to flower, followed by an orange and black monarch and then a lilting white creature with green-marbled wings. The three friends floated from zinnias to hyacinths to daisies, landing on my butterfly, bush where they feasted on sweet flower nectar.

As I observed these lilting creatures, I wished I were as carefree as they were.

I knew they hadn't always been as they are now. They had begun life as tiny eggs, maturing into caterpillars and outgrowing their skin five times. I knew it must have taken great energy for them to create the fragile but durable chrysalis protection they had lived in for a time in their early life.

I wondered what it would be like to be constricted and imprisoned by an outer protection that had grown too small.

These delicate but tenacious creatures had created their own constraints, regenerating themselves from their beginnings. The twisting, the pressing, the pushing and struggle to discard their shackles. What exhausting work!

And in the process they had become more beautiful than the tiny egg or inching caterpillar could have dreamed possible. The trials, the incubation, the hard work, and the perseverance earned them a reward of beauty and freedom which they share with those around them. A reward they wouldn't have appreciated had they not known confinement first.

The three friends darted off to another flower bed.

I sat back in my chair to enjoy their dance. As I watched, I reflected on the parallels between their lives and mine. As a youth I devised protection to shield me from harm. I worked hard to keep my defense in place as I related to the world around me. But as difficulties came my way, I grew and changed. I pushed against my cocoon. Many times my way of looking at life had become a prison. I learned how to develop wings and fly. Now I can flit from flower to flower and enjoy the freedom I have found. Sometimes I slip back into my chrysalis, but I find my wings again rather quickly.

Fly with me. Find your wings and come along. The journey is spectacular.

> *"We delight in the beauty of the butterfly, but rarely admit the changes it has gone through to achieve that beauty."*
>
> —Maya Angelou

Refuge comes in many disguises: depression, self-deprecation, or inability to act. It has a thousand faces. You have developed your own safeguards unique to you. An abundant life can be yours, but you must identify and release the obstructions that keep wisdom and wealth from you.

The purpose of this book is to discuss a step-by-step course to expand your optimistic thinking and to enhance your ability to give and receive.

Be proactive so that you can grow with positive energy. Become the best you. Release your protective prisons.

Each chapter in the book will enable you to develop a program to discard your defenses. Since your personal defenses are unique, you will need to tailor the healing to work for you.

May abundant blessings come to you in this quest. Allow God or your higher power into your life, and find the key to open yourself up and access new dreams and visions. Reach for the stars with positive energy.

How to use this book:

At the beginning of each chapter a negative statement is written. "What I don't want" is sometimes easier to think of than "What I do want." Take the negative statement at the start of each chapter and turn it into a positive for yourself. Begin a journal just for this purpose. It will be a great place for you to write your thoughts and memories also. Tailor your writing to your needs and review it often. Write your positive affirmations, and as you think about them, say them, and begin to believe them. You'll draw the light and optimism to you.

The overview steps at the end of each chapter are not necessarily a summary of the chapter but a sample to-do list that will aid you in recording your own inventory and setting your own goals.

How many of us read self-help books and get enthused about setting goals, only to feel overwhelmed and discard them after a few months? This book isn't just something to read—it's interactive. Examine it from cover to cover if you wish, but then go back and work chapter by chapter—as you have time—to bring positive influences into your life.

Part 1

Prescription for Work Ethic

As I have worked with people over the years, I have been fascinated by the different ways people order their lives. Some waft with the wind and others try to control every minute detail of the circumstances that surround them. Many that approach life in these extreme ways tend to give up their goals if they don't succeed the first time.

People who do find success usually have a dogged determination to make their goals happen. We cheer these tenacious people on because they give us hope.

One of the reasons we love fictional characters so much is because we anticipate their success. Many great novelists employ a secret called the "try-fail" cycle. The protagonist must <u>fail twice before he finally finds the courage to succeed</u>. We cheer our hero on because he has failed and fought back until he finds prosperity.

I like using this model in my own life. After I experience failure, I realize that my life is not over—it will not be the death of me. I dig deep inside myself, determined to overcome, and then, when I do finally accomplish my goal, it's all the sweeter.

In the end it's not the failure or success that's important. It's the process that makes you who you are. <u>Courage, determination,</u> and <u>fortitude</u> are the keys to taking your life in the direction you want it to go.

Chapter 1

Long-Term Goals

I do not want to wait to see what happens without having a plan.

Aristotle defined our connectedness to goals as follows: "Man is a goal-seeking animal. His life only has meaning if he is reaching out and striving for his goals." Become excited about the direction you want your life to take. Find a path that will bring you joy and happiness. Be the artist of your own painting.

We Become What We Think

All of us participate in goal setting whether on a conscious or subconscious level.

> "We are shaped by our thoughts. We become what we think."
> — Buddha

Samantha, age seventeen, came to therapy for depression. She constantly described herself as large and chubby. Words like this were so much a part of her thought process that she wasn't even aware of her negative thinking. She had become what she thought about. She even bought her clothes a size too big because she was so ashamed of her shape. For Samantha to change her life, she had to set a long-term goal to change her thinking.

Become aware of your own thoughts just like Samantha did. Are they positive or negative? Do you like them as they are, or would you like to change them? Keep the positive and release the negative. Proactively decide the direction you want your life to take so you're not swept along with the daily tide of life.

Target Long-Term Objectives

Goals don't have to be set at the beginning of the year. Be creative and willing to think outside the box. Look at your life: when is the best time for you to set and evaluate your goals? If you are a student or a teacher, is fall a better time to assess your situation? If you own a business, you may want to set goals and marketing strategies right before the holidays. Only you can know what is best for you.

Individuals, couples, and groups can take vacation time away from daily routines to establish goals. I know a circle of friends who get together once a year to discuss the progress they have made toward their goals and to set new ones. Attending workshops or conferences is another great time to set priorities.

Life gets busy and complicated. We may be pulled in various directions. Many of us follow through with our goals for a while, but then other things cloud our vision and we lose sight of them. What can we do to improve our consistency?

Be Aware of Your Patterns

We need to be alert to our mode of planning. Look at past calendars and journals. What do you like about the way you set goals? What would you alter? List the changes you want to make and put them in a prominent place where you'll see them often. Review them carefully at a routine time, like the first day of each month.

> "Let me tell you the secret that has led me to my goal: my strength lies solely in my tenacity."
>
> Louis Pasteur

What distractions take you off task? Vacations, holidays, family visits, houseguests, time with friends? But what if instead of looking at these as distractions, you incorporated them into your plan? Make them part of your long-term goals. If the unexpected visit of houseguests interrupts your weekly service goal, include the assistance you give your unplanned visitors as a substitute. Distractions can be incorporated into your successes if you include them in your long-term program.

Involve Others in Your Goals

Taking time for reflection can be personal, but it can also be done in a group setting. Include others in your objectives. If reading is one of your goals, read a good book with family or friends. Form a book club. You'll not only meet your reading goal, but you'll develop great friendships along the way. Goals concerning food lend themselves to a group effort. The philosophy of positive thinking can yield success if incorporated in a family situation, with friends, or in the workplace. Sharing goals with others gives us additional support—and often facilitates friendships.

Discussing your goals with those around you makes your commitment greater, because someone else knows about it. It makes you accountable to someone and gives you great support. Many times those around you have similar goals and are willing to share in your struggles and successes. They may also be willing to give you valuable observations that will advance your progress.

Two heads are always better than one. Ask for feedback from others and brainstorm ideas for goal completion. It's great to listen to ideas from those around you. It will expand your list of possibilities and give you lots of choices for setting your plan of action.

Be Flexible When You Plan

<u>Be open to change. It's consistently part of life.</u>

A young, single client, Sophia, owned a thriving catering business. To manage her time, she tried setting personal goals, including things both at work and in her outside life. Often, she felt frustrated because she couldn't accomplish her plan. Some days she didn't have time to work out as she wished, and her reading goal had to be cut out all together when business got too busy. She was always at work. Holidays, religious celebrations, weddings—as much as she loved her job, the hectic schedule it imposed was usurping all of her personal time. How could she be consistent? How could she keep up?

She struggled as she shared her dilemma with me, but eventually she came up with a plan. She laid out her yearly calendar, assessed the previous year's volume of business for each month, and set her objectives accordingly. During the busy months she developed a short list of goals. For example, she kept her spiritual reading to fifteen minutes a day, and she spent her lunchtime at the gym. When work slowed down, she spent an hour in spiritual study and meditation, and she completed a full-body workout at the gym after work hours.

Sophia is in the busy season of her life's work. As her business grows, she can add employees and restructure her time as she wishes. Evaluation, brainstorming, and follow-through help Sophia consistently set her short-term goals in order for her to accomplish her long-term plans.

Choose Your Goals Thoughtfully

"People with goals succeed because they know where they're going."
Earl Nightingale

Goal setting can be difficult. I have a young friend who couldn't decide on a major in college, so she never set long-term goals. During her first two years of school, she floated from English to physics to business to veterinary medicine to, finally, prelaw. When I first saw her in a counseling setting, all she could do was berate herself for wasting her time and her money. She considered dropping out of school altogether just because she couldn't make a decision.

As we talked about her situation, she decided to take a semester off and visit experts in the vocations she thought might be interesting. Then she could return to school with a plan in mind, one she knew she really wanted to explore.

After some introspection, she reframed her lack of focus into a period of discovery. She let go of her guilt because she knew that this decision wasn't one she should make lightly. She'd be working in her chosen field for at least thirty years, and it needed to be something she loved.

She decided to study every possibility carefully before setting her long-term goals.

Goals May Change

It's healthy for you to amend your desires as you progress through life. Some of your goals at age twenty will not be the same at age sixty. Enjoy the ride along the way and readjust when you find it necessary.

When I was a young mother, my children seemed to consume me. When they became more self-sufficient, I returned to school and accomplished my goal to become a therapist. Now, as a grandmother, I'm able to pursue writing interests. I love this time of life and am grateful to have the opportunity to balance my time between family and personal goals.

Evaluate your place in life and look at your big picture. Be proactive in the direction you want your life to take. Set your long-term goals and fill your days with short-term goals that match what you want to become. Be sure to enjoy each step along the way.

Set a Definite Priority Each Day

If you find yourself starting out great and then letting the goals fall by the wayside, get back to your program. *Evaluate your progress at a set time each month.* Remember, we're all inconsistent at times. As you assess your progress, adjust your course so you stay on track.

The tiny egg clung to the underside of the milkweed. She looked up at the beautiful creatures fluttering on the branches above. Here she was, trapped in this tiny shell with wax protection. Could she ever become as elegant and beautiful as the butterflies above her? The egg dreamed of becoming that beautiful. She set her goal, certain she would be able to achieve it. Her vision was clear. One day she would fly free.

Devise your long-term goals. Keep them ever in your vision as the tiny egg does—you are in the process of becoming free.

Internal Joy Is the Key to Success

Overview Steps:

- Set yearly goals
- Set monthly goals
  - Make a subheading for each month with specific goals
  - Plan in holidays and work schedules as part of the goal setting
- Set a time of accounting for yourself
- Ask for feedback
- Understand that goals may change
- Follow through
- Put your list where you can see it
- Be consistent in your efforts
- If you slack off, focus back on your long-term goals

Chapter 2

Short-Term Goals

I do not want to live without a plan.

Write a positive statement that you can use as an affirmation. Affirmative thoughts and declarations repeated over and over can make your life more positive, just as negative thoughts can pull you down.

You set short-term goals whether you think you do or not. If you don't proactively plan a direction for your day when you get up in the morning, your idleness will send you wherever your thoughts go.

Short-term goals complete long-term goals.

> "The man who moves a mountain begins by carrying away small stones."
>
> *Confucius*

To move along the path of long-term goals, create stepping-stones of short-term actions. Make yourself a list and cross off each task as you complete it. Plan, plan, plan.

The Need for Constancy

There is a continuum for constancy, and each of us must find our own comfort zone.

Some people border on compulsiveness in the rigidity of their daily routine. Normally, when the words 'compulsive' and 'rigid' are used, negative connotations come to mind. At times these people are also called neurotic, or obsessive, but this may not be the case.

Sometimes I find myself at this end of the continuum. I like my house picked up, and my husband teases me that I clean up the dinner dishes before the food's cold. He says I'm obsessed with cleaning, but I don't feel that way. It's just a habit I've gotten into, and I'm comfortable with it, so it doesn't detract from the positive energy I feel.

Your feelings create the energy around you.

At the other end of the continuum are those free spirits who thrive on going with the flow and being spontaneous. I have an artist friend who works this way. She couldn't create if she structured her days in rigidity.

Most of us probably find our place somewhere between these two extremes. I may be more task-oriented than my friend, but that's my way, and it's comfortable for me. However, if I don't factor in some creative time, my life becomes frustrating and dull. My friend may be more artistic and free-spirited, and that works for her. She's a wonderful artist, and her commissions can be sizable. But if she doesn't have some kind of an agenda, she won't finish her painting on time to collect that commission.

Establish Weekly and Daily Work Patterns

"The daily grind of hard work gets a person polished."
Unknown

Keep yourself organized with a list that's somewhat prioritized. Post it on the bathroom mirror or the fridge—somewhere you often look. You may work on your plan five days a week, giving yourself the weekend off. At times, you may work at night or on the weekends to complete specific goals you can't accomplish during the day.

To begin, keep a task journal in a small pocket notebook. Record each task with the following four components.

- Time
- Task
- Feeling (as you're working at the task)
- Completion

This will assist you in identifying your work pattern and the feelings that either aid you or prevent you from accomplishing your goals. This system is rather time consuming, so use it only until you discover the problems with the way you work. I only employ it when I'm having trouble completing my work, because this method helps me identify what's holding me back.

Here's an example of what your journal might look like:

8:00 a.m./housekeeping/depressed/task not accomplished

8:30 a.m./meditation/peace/task accomplished

6:30 p.m./work out/exhilarated/task accomplished

After you find your overall daily style, look for specific task completion patterns to see how you accomplish individual tasks.

As you identify your behaviors, look for the tasks that draw positive energy into your life. Sometimes you may find negative energy associated with the process. If this is the case, look for the individual jobs that call up that negativity.

Emotional Triggers

Emotional triggers can be defined as the tasks, situations, or experiences that carry negative feelings from your youth or childhood. When you find yourself feeling pessimistic or depressed, write about it. Allow yourself to feel this energy. Think back to the earliest time you experienced that feeling. Write about it. Then release the negative energy and replace it with positive feelings.

For instance, work before play was instilled into me so strongly as a child that I have a difficult time playing until all the work is done. Sometimes it isn't possible to finish all the tasks at once. I've learned that even if I take some time off, the work will still be there. It's fine to take a break and then get back on the job without feeling guilty. We need a break at times to keep our minds fresh and to maintain positive energy in our jobs. Both work and play can be available without any associated negativity.

After I recognized my emotional triggers and identified the time when the "have to" feelings about work began in my life, I allowed myself to feel those negative feelings and then release them. I still do this today. My favorite ways of letting them go are visualizing myself relaxing, laughing, and enjoying lunch with friends. I can now take time each day to do something fun by using positive affirmations like

- I will have time to complete this task tomorrow.
- I find joy in doing something for myself.
- I take pleasure in time with others.
- Laughter releases my tension.

I let go of the guilt and the tension I feel inside, and I begin to replace those negative feelings with positive ones that fit with my affirmations.

As you find your emotional triggers, use Part D of this book, "Practicing the Process," to establish a specific plan for healing that will work for you.

I had a client, Jane, whose mother was fastidious about cleaning. Cooking spices were alphabetized and placed on the shelves by date. Knives and forks had to be lined up in the drawer, and clothes and shoes in the closet were color coded. Jane remembers housecleaning as a time of criticism and anger, when tension between her and her mother would escalate.

As an adult, Jane had a difficult time creating order in her house because of her negative feelings. After Jane discovered the emotional triggers from her childhood, she wrote about those experiences. Then, as she did her housework, she used positive energy exercises like visualization and self-talk. Soon the positive energy she felt paired with the cleaning and erased much of her childhood negativity.

During this process, Jane began to choose to live in an upbeat environment and was able to accomplish her goals in this area. She didn't have a choice as a child, but as an adult she did. By using constructive energy and restructuring her thought patterns, she is now able to keep a clean home, and enjoy doing so!

After you find the triggers in your own life, give thanks for the help they have given you. Jane later expressed an appreciation for her cleaning problems because she grew personally during the process of letting the negativity go. She developed internal strength that she would not have found if she hadn't had the problem in the first place. Challenges in life can bring us blessings.

"Oh Lord, who lends me life, lend me a heart replete with thankfulness."

Shakespeare

One Step at a Time

If you feel overwhelmed by your tasks, take a step back and focus on one small job at a time. I do this to keep myself from feeling like I'm drowning. After I rid myself of the negative feelings, I think of something positive.

For instance, when my husband and I were installing closet doors in our basement bedroom, we had problems with the first door, which hung crookedly and wouldn't shut. We both felt overwhelmed. If we had problems with all the doors like we did with this one, we'd never get finished. I suggested we start on a new door that didn't have any problems, but he felt we needed to troubleshoot the dilemma to build our confidence so we could continue to hang the rest of them. He remeasured the door and trimmed it to fit the opening, and before long, it shut perfectly. That sense of accomplishment was just the boost we needed, and soon we had all the doors installed. Not only was the task achieved, but we felt more confident in the work we had done.

Make a Realistic Schedule

A busy mother may make a list of ten goals and only be able to accomplish four or five of them. This is because when you have children, other priorities come into play, like forgotten lunches, soccer games, book reports, or countless other things. She may alter her list of goals to include the lunches and soccer games. She knows her children are the most important priority.

Similarly, a busy executive may make a list of ten goals and only accomplish a few of them because of a business trip, workshops, or a meeting with the boss. He or she may add the business trips and workshops into his or her goals.

In order to be consistent, it's important to take into account the expected and unexpected barriers that always come up. Include them in your goals. Be flexible enough to know that the people in your life are most important, and they are not always predictable.

Evaluate Your Progress Often

It's fine to read through this book and get excited about your goals, but how do you sustain long-lasting change? Thinking and behavioral patterns are habitual. For most people, it takes several weeks to change a habit. The first thing I do when I decide to change a habit is review the proactive feelings I have when I set my goals. Writing a description of your feelings when you set your objectives will help. Then as you refer back to it, you'll remember exactly how you felt and why.

Each week I refer to my feeling journal to put myself in the frame of mind I was in when I set my goals. Then I evaluate my progress and modify my aspirations.

Pair this process with something you love to do. I evaluate my improvement each week on Sunday afternoon before I let myself read a novel, something I love to do. Take this idea and modify it to meet your needs. Be creative.

Post your list where you will see it often. Pair a "have to" with a "want to." Finish a short-term goal before you go to a movie. Be flexible enough to accomplish what you can and allow it to be sufficient. You are enough just as you are.

> *"I am only one, but still I am one. I cannot do everything, but still I can do something. I will not refuse to do the something I can do."*
> *Helen Keller*

The tiny egg is developing into a gray caterpillar, changing and growing. Each day she has a small goal to become more—every aspiration leading to her vision of the butterfly she will someday become. She pokes her tiny head out of the protective egg sac and looks around, eating milkweed and gaining strength, intent on her dream.

Keep your long-term goal ever in mind, seeking it daily by means of your short-term goals. Use them as stepping stones up the hill of your dreams, never losing sight of your desire.

Innate Enjoyment Is the Fulcrum of Self-Attainment

Overview Steps:

- Journal your daily schedule
  - Time
  - Task
  - Feelings
  - Completion
- Look for emotional triggers
- Look for patterns you wish to change
- Look for patterns you wish to keep
- Look for emotional triggers that keep you stuck
- Set tasks that can be accomplished
- Post a list where you will see it
- Set a work time
- Step back if you feel overwhelmed
- Work at one small task until it is done
- See yourself as successful
- Remember that feelings will build on themselves
- Infuse yourself with positive energy
- Allow days when tasks are not accomplished because of other priorities

Chapter 3

Alleviating Procrastination

I do not want to be a procrastinator.

Write an affirmation. Fill yourself with positive energy.

> *"What may be done at any time will be done at no time."*
> *Scottish Proverb*

Procrastination blocks positive energy. Has there ever been a time when you didn't get to the things on your list that you really wanted to do? Did you feel frustrated or angry?

Goodness is all around in the positive energy field you create.

Reba and her husband had been looking forward to their dream cruise of the Greek Islands for over a year. Reba knew she had some bills to pay and laundry to do before they left, but she put off doing them until the evening before their flight to Rome. She worked late into the night—feeling a lot of stress. The next morning she dragged herself out of bed and was late getting ready. She and her husband argued all the way to the airport. Heavy traffic and long security lines added to her anxiety, and they almost missed their flight.

Reba began the trip with negative energy, which seemed to spread to everything around her. The struggle to regain positive energy haunted her for several days. She temporarily lost the blessing of serenity because she put things off. From then on, she determined to stop this pattern in her life. She began to see the blueprint of her behavior and gradually started gaining peace back into her life.

How did Reba change her behavior? She began by pairing a positive task with one she didn't want to do. She made herself get the laundry done before she went shopping. She posted little notes to jog her mind back to the peace and serenity she wanted. Changes didn't happen all at once, but slowly, over time. She remained grateful for the negative energy that filled her before her cruise. She says it was one of her greatest gifts because it led to her goal of joy and tranquility.

> "An obstacle may either be a stepping stone or a stumbling block. It's your choice."
>
> Unknown

Being a Perfectionist

Isabella was a perfectionist. She fell into a common procrastination trap of putting off a project until the last minute so she had an excuse for not being perfect. She knew if she waited until the last minute she didn't have to do her best. She could tell herself she could have done better if she had taken her time.

Isabella's manager gave her a project to complete by the end of the week. Isabella wanted to impress her boss, and she worried all week about the task, but she didn't start the project until the day before it was due. Because she procrastinated, she had to stay up all night finishing it.

The next day at work she was tired but relieved because she'd completed the assignment. However, there were some glaring flaws in her work because she'd left it to the last minute, and her boss was disappointed. Isabella left work that night with a knot in her stomach. She hated feeling like a failure, but it was something she'd experienced all of her life.

This incident was a gift for Isabella. She reflected back to the first time she felt worthless and related several childhood incidents that mirrored her present-day feelings. She purchased a feeling journal and wrote about her apprehension. Then she replaced her negative statements with positive affirmations.

Childhood Beliefs	Adult Affirmation
I am never good enough.	I am wonderful.
I am inadequate.	I am a miraculous human being.
I carry shame wherever I am.	I carry positive energy and love with me always.

After completing this task, she said a positive spark began to grow inside her. It was as if the child inside her needed someone to tell her she was good and capable.

Isabella continued the positive affirmations and could feel herself heal inside each time she said them. She felt like a new person and began to change her behavior one step at a time. The next time her boss gave her a project, she began it right away. Her work quality improved and so did her relationship with herself and her boss.

Being Too Task Oriented

Olivia was very thorough at her job. She worked from home as a medical transcriptionist for a local psychiatrist. She was always late when she went to pick her children up from school or take them to a doctor's appointment because she had to finish "just one more" dictation. She scolded and berated herself for focusing on small tasks instead of looking at the big picture of her entire day.

Besides being too task oriented, Olivia was easily distracted. She loved to read about the cases she typed. Many times she would get caught up in researching a topic and lose all track of time. She felt like a child when her husband had to call her from work to remind her of her schedule.

Olivia didn't want to feel like a child anymore. She wanted to change her behavior, so she used her calendar and phone reminders to help her focus. She wrote several affirmations that helped her change her thinking.

- I am responsible.
- I am on time.
- I enjoy a schedule.
- I care for my family.

Olivia began to look at her daily schedule as a whole. She worked until her phone reminded her to pick up the kids. Since she loved to research the cases she typed, she gave herself permission to study their particulars further each evening. Her relationship with her husband improved because she had transformed herself from the role of a child who needed to be reminded of things to that of an adult who could take care of herself.

Feeling Guilt and Anxiety

A client, Sally, reported feeling guilty and anxious in all aspects of her life. She came into therapy because her life felt "out of order." She wanted a clean house, but she never got around to it. Her bank accounts were never balanced, because it took too much effort. She sat in my office and cried because she was overwhelmed. As she kept a journal, she could see her pattern. Procrastination kept her anxious and in a state of chaos. Guilt seemed to fill her chest so that she could hardly breathe because she had left many tasks incomplete. She chose to change the negativity this behavior gave her by visualizing the way she wanted it to be.

Visualizing is making a picture in your mind. Think of a movie you have just watched. Imagine the scene that was the scariest. Now picture the most beautiful landscape. Envision the funniest part of the movie. You are visualizing. Creating pictures in your mind is like daydreaming. It can be relaxing, positive, and fun.

As Sally visualized a neater house, her actions followed her thoughts. Before she left for work, she began to do a quick gathering of things so the house was neat when she came home from work. She noticed a drastic difference in her energy level when the house was straightened up.

Letting go of the negative was uncomfortable at first, but through positive imagery and encouraging self-talk she was able to accomplish her goals.

Sally congratulated herself when she could see the changes. A pat on the back seemed like she was fibbing to herself at first, but she kept doing it. The positive visualization and self-talk felt better the more she used it.

Being Counter-Dependent

At times, young people rebel against authority. They grow up with patterns of counter-dependency rather than becoming independent. Counter-dependency means acting against someone or something rather than for oneself. If teens get stuck in this pattern, they can carry it with them into adulthood.

Amber was an intelligent young woman. She knew if she argued with her mother over household chore assignments, her mother would lose her temper, then feel guilty, and do the task herself. Amber's pattern of getting out of work continued throughout her teenage years. However, when Amber tried to use this tactic as a young adult on her boss, she was fired from her job. She came into therapy devastated and scared because she had rent to pay and food to buy and didn't know how. She wanted to be independent.

Amber's friendly personality and good communication skills landed her another job right away. But she panicked about losing it. Even when she came to understand the difference between counter-dependence and true independence, she still wondered if she could be successful.

She wrote a list of goals in her computer at work and looked at it often. The list went something like this:
- I can listen to my boss.
- I can begin a task immediately.
- I am a hard worker.
- I can take care of myself.

Amber needed time to change her behavior. She knew it took a few weeks to change a habit, but she was motivated to keep her job and turned her actions around quickly at work. At her apartment, she had to push herself a little harder to complete certain tasks because no one was watching. She left dirty dishes in the sink for days, until ants found their way into the leftover food on the plates.

It was a struggle for Amber to teach herself to be independent, but she was grateful for the struggle because she received the blessings of self-discipline.

Discover Your Behavior Pattern

Study your procrastination patterns. All behaviors have a payoff. Negative behaviors have negative payoffs such as crisis, guilt, anxiety, and nervousness. Positive behaviors elicit positive payoffs like peace, serenity, and feelings of accomplishment. Look inward and journal your behavior to see what the payoff is for your procrastinating behavior. Let yourself feel the negativity inside. Then write about it.

> "Waiting is a trap. There will always be reasons to wait. The truth is, there are only two things in life, reasons and results, and the reasons simply don't count."
>
> Dr. Robert Anthony

Create positive affirmations and visualizations concerning your negativity as is best for you. Pair a task you don't enjoy doing with one you love. Generate optimistic energy and your life will be blessed.

Release procrastination into the light to be healed. There are many other therapeutic methods that will work. Look in chapter 6 (Healing Fear) to find the ones that appeal to you.

The tiny caterpillar has broken free of her egg sac, using it for nourishment and growth. No more putting off her goals—she becomes an eating and growing entity.

You, likewise, have laid aside the procrastinating habits of the past and are moving forward toward light and positive energy—to become the elegant creature of your dreams.

Internal Commitment Is the Key to Achievement

Overview Steps:

- Keep a thought journal
- Look for a pattern in your behavior
- Find the negative payoff:
  - Excitement
  - Anxiety
  - Guilt
- Pair a positive task with one you are likely to procrastinate
- Use positive self-talk
- Use positive visualization
- Add any methods from chapter 6 that you like

Chapter 4

Being Responsible for Life Choices

I don't want to blame others for my problems.

Some people tend to fault others for their state of affairs. They are angry at life and feel sorry for themselves. Rather than taking responsibility for their circumstances, they blame outside sources for their problems. Some may be irritated with God because He doesn't fix their life. Others may be overwhelmed by health problems and seek pity because of them. Some may see other external sources as the root of their troubles.

A Perfect Life

I had clients of varying religious backgrounds who came to therapy angry with God because He didn't make their lives perfect. They were active in their religion and didn't understand why God didn't fix their troubled marriage, take away the grief of a family death, or rescue them from an addiction. God will not rescue you as if you were a small child. As an adult, you are responsible to act rather than be acted upon. You must learn to be proactive and strive to solve your problems. Sometimes you can do it alone, or you may need the help of others—including religious leaders if you so choose—but no one will take away your ability to act for yourself. No one will "fix" you without some effort on your part.

Andrea sought counseling because her minister recommended it after her husband left her to run off to Mexico with his secretary. She was in crisis, but she was sure God would take her problems away if she were just more righteous. She believed things were going badly in her life because she was not as good as she could be.

Andrea had a difficult time coming to terms with the fact that she would need to find a place to live and a job to provide for herself and her children rather than waiting for God to take care of her.

Since she was a Christian, we talked about James 2:17–20 in the New Testament.

> *"Even so faith, if it hath not works, is dead, being alone. . . . But wilt thou know, O vain man, that faith without works is dead?"*
> *James 2:17–20*

Andrea began to realize that she couldn't just sit back and wait for someone—even God—to fix her problem. God would bless her, but she had to do the work herself. Since she had a good education, she filled out applications immediately and quickly found a teaching position.

She met with her minister often, and he guided her through this new perspective of her relationship with God. She developed a positive attitude about life. Peace entered her heart as she learned to be solution focused—thankful for the gift of responsibility.

Becoming Proactive

Several clients left therapy, unable to understand the concept of caring for themselves. Some turned away from their religion because God didn't solve their problems. Disenchantment filled their lives, when they could have had the blessings of light and love.

I wish these people well. I hope that someday the light of proactivity will shine in their lives, and they will begin to change on the inside, rather than looking for some external force to change them on the outside.

> *"Man must cease attributing his problems to his environment, and learn again to exercise his will—his personal responsibility."*
> *Dr. Albert Schweitzer*

Our Attitude and Health Problems

Sometimes people feel sorry for themselves, focusing on their illnesses or troubles. When I was visiting in a distant city, I had lunch with an old acquaintance, Hilda. I had lost touch with her for over twenty years, except for the yearly Christmas letter.

Hilda had many health problems, and the doctors told her she needed back surgery, but she didn't trust physicians. Her paranoia caused her to believe they would do her more harm than good.

Hilda seemed preoccupied with her poor health and it filtered into other areas of her life. It kept her stuck and unable to fulfill her goals. She hadn't done any traveling since we were young and couldn't work because of her poor physical condition. She was disappointed with life and trapped by her physical problems. Because of her negative thinking, she was stuck in an unfulfilled life.

Alice's story had a different ending. She was diagnosed with multiple sclerosis, and yet her life became more meaningful and positive than it had been before the sickness, simply because of how she handled it.

Alice came into therapy shortly after she discovered her disease. She was on heavy medication once a month and had to be very careful with her lifestyle. She slept more than usual and sat down to rest in a chair every time she passed one. She had difficulty getting around because the medication made her dizzy. She used a cane since she felt unsteady on her feet. She often dropped things because her arms and hands tingled and went numb. Depression haunted her.

Alice had every reason to feel sorry for herself and give up, but she was a spunky little lady, who loved life too much to let it go.

Her negative situation didn't get her down. She worked with her doctor to regulate her medication, instead of against him, like Hilda. Determined to shake the depression, she kept a gratitude journal. Each day she listed the physical successes she had. She was happy when she could just clear the dinner table or make her favorite beef stew. She looked for the positive in her life. Her gratitude journal contained page after page of seemingly insignificant items, like thankfulness for being able to feel the blades of grass beneath her bare feet or to watch colorful autumn leaves flutter from the trees.

Alice structured her days so that she saw friends when she could. Reading to her grandchildren and doing simple art projects with them highlighted her life. She and her husband had always wanted to travel when he retired, but instead they decided to do it now, while Alice was still able. They are currently planning a trip around the world.

Her hopelessness lifted with antidepressants and a positive thinking program. She inspired those around her, including me. She is truly a blessing to her friends and family members by showing them the way to live life and face hardships.

"Some pursue happiness—others create it."
Ralph Waldo Emerson

Walk Down Another Street

There have been times when I found myself with a problem. I realized that I got myself into my dilemma because of some of the decisions I had made. Since I could see my part, I knew I could make some different choices and get myself out of my situation.

I looked at my life and brainstormed a long list of things I wanted to change. I looked at these one at a time to eliminate negativity from my life. I learned to live life in a different way.

It took several years of day-by-day work, but I got out of my predicament. Maybe you have heard the parable of the hole that is used in AA meetings:

> *I walk down the street and fall in a hole.*
> *I don't know how I got in.*
> *It is hard to find my way out.*
>
> *I walk down the street and see the hole.*
> *I fall in it anyway.*
> *I have been in the hole before and know how to get out.*
>
> *I walk down the street and see the hole.*
> *This time I walk around it.*
> *I just walk down another street.*

If spending money is your hole, walk down another street by getting involved with Debtors Anonymous, or taking a money management class at your local community college. If arguing with a spouse is your black pit, find another road by calling a therapist or attending a marriage seminar.

Jed and Clarissa argued all the time. When they came into therapy I asked them to write down the step-by-step process of their fights. It was a difficult assignment, and it took them several fights before they were able to complete it.

First, Jed would ask Clarissa a question she really couldn't answer, like "Why would your mother do a thing like that?"

Next, Clarissa would answer the question to the best of her ability. Then Jed would begin to argue with her about the answer she gave.

When they could see the pattern, they were able to stop it. They "walked down another street." Instead of getting angry, they began to laugh over their disagreements. This brought them closer together and enriched their relationship.

We Attract What We Think About

Those who are angry fill themselves with negative energy and bring the things they dislike into their lives by focusing on them. Center your attention and energy on the things you want, not the things you dislike. Mother Teresa has said she would never attend an anti-war rally, but if a pro-peace rally were held, she would gladly attend.

Bring about change by working for the things you want. My daughter had a young high school friend in southern California who didn't like people swearing on his school campus, so he organized a no-swearing club.

As a young person, he's already changing the world, and this change is now spreading around the country.

> "Life is a gift, and it offers us the privilege, opportunity, and responsibility to give something back by becoming more."
>
> *Anthony Robbins*

If you find yourself in a place you don't want to be:
- Take a deep breath
- Look at the decisions and actions that brought you to this place
- Take responsibility for them and decide how you want to change
- Make a list of the things you want to be different in your life
- Come up with solutions for each one
- Begin one at a time to do things differently
- Walk down another street

That other street has changed my life, and it's a great feeling.

The tiny caterpillar is eating voraciously and growing—now responsible for her life choices. She knows she must nourish herself in order to evolve. She glances toward the ground. It's a long way down, and she doesn't want to fall. She is careful to keep a firm grasp on the branch to stay safe, propelling herself toward her vision.

You are like this busy little hard-working creature. Life choices are clear to you as you seek the positive energy of the world. Each day peace becomes your companion, bringing wholeness to your being.

Inward Solace Is a Blueprint of Wholeness

Overview Steps:
- Journal your thinking pattern
- Take responsibility for your situations in life
- Put positive energy into your life
  - Brainstorm ways you want to change
  - Develop a plan of steps to get out of negative situations
  - Practice walking down another street
- Look at your specific situation
  - Write down each step of an argument
  - Find the pattern in it
  - Record another argument and see if the pattern repeats itself
  - Choose another way to communicate
- Be vigilant to keep from falling into old patterns

Part 2

Approach to Self-Care

No one comes from a perfect background. Positive and negative experiences belong to all of us. My clients taught me a lot about pain and abuse in life. Some of them felt victimized by the hazards of their lives. Others grew strong from their affliction.

I found that the difference in these two outlooks on life came from the attitude of each person—their disposition, posture, and point of view.

I have often asked myself how I apply this principle in my own life. Do I let the negative happenings in my life send me down the path of adverse thinking, or can I see the gift in each of these experiences?

Many times I hear parents tell their children they need an attitude adjustment, but sometimes I'm the one who needs to alter my perspective through reading uplifting quotes, listening to soothing music, enjoying beautiful art, or just sitting quietly so I can hear my innermost thoughts and wishes.

Life happens to all of us. It's what you do with those happenings that makes you who you are.

Chapter 5

The Gifts of an Imperfect Life

I do not want to have any problems.

I don't want to deal with problems. Why can't my life be perfect? I wish everything would always go my way.

My friend and I joke that if we were in charge of the world, we'd have no problems at all. We'd make life simple and easy. Unfortunately, things don't work that way. We all have problems, and they help us mature.

We only grow if we are solution focused.

The Perfect Facade

From the outside, Janice looked like she had the perfect life—a great job, good friends, and a nice place to live. But Janice was living a double life. She had maxed out all of her credit cards, and every month she worried about having enough money to pay her rent.

Janice's mother was proud that Janice had an ideal life, so Janice couldn't tell her mother how things really were. She couldn't share her problems with her friends either. She needed to appear perfect.

At age twenty-five, Janice came into therapy very depressed, wanting someone to fix her problems. However, she soon realized that she had gotten herself into this situation, and only she could get herself out.

Janice's lack of self-esteem drove her to live a lie, and she alone could change her circumstances by being honest. She thought that people wouldn't like her if she didn't have the best of everything. She believed they wouldn't want to be her friend unless she bought them dinners and gifts.

Janice had never been taught to manage money, and she hadn't taken the initiative to learn on her own. I helped her find a financial counselor. She looked at the frivolous ways she spent money—buying too many clothes and picking up the tab at lunch too often. She began to live within her means and to pay herself first, to build up some savings.

Janice had to find a cheaper place to live, so she needed to inform her family and friends. Her fear about telling others seemed to paralyze her. In order to become confident enough to let go of the facade, she wrote positive affirmations:

- Others are supportive of me when I am honest.
- Honesty releases my anxiety.
- It takes courage to be honest. I am courageous.
- I love myself enough to be authentic.
- My friends will like me if I am genuine.

She repeated her affirmations several times a day, and her self-assurance grew.

She told her two closest girlfriends about her problems, and they understood.

Janice began to feel relieved as she shared her true self. Her friends liked her better without the pretense.

However, she worried about telling her mother she'd moved to a new apartment, certain that her mother would be hurt and ashamed of her. Janice decided to explain things during a therapy session. She didn't think her mother would get too upset in front of me.

The meeting was a very powerful one. (Sessions with adult children and parents are usually a wonderful way to open up communication.)

Her mother listened to Janice's explanation of her troubles. She told Janice she appreciated her honesty and said she understood. She also shared that she had had similar money problems as a youth, and she talked about the solutions she had found.

As a result of the therapy session, both Janice and her mother were able to let go of the perfection pretense and be real with each other. She and her mother became much better friends and really began to fully enjoy each other's company.

Janice's money problems were not solved overnight, but she now walked the road to financial competence. More importantly, she lived a real life—not pretending anymore.

Skewed Perspective

Geraldine came into my office depressed. She had a secret about her husband that she was ashamed to share—no one had a problem like she did. I didn't press her for information; I just let her talk because I could see it was difficult for her to get the words out.

As the interview progressed, she was finally able to say that her husband was a cross-dresser. She felt violated. She never knew when her unmentionables would be missing from her drawers and closet and when they were, she knew her husband was out "parading around" (as she called it) with his friends.

She'd tried telling him how she hated having him wear her things. He told her this was his way of releasing tension. He said he got a euphoric high each time he met his friends to go dancing.

We talked about him taking her clothes, and then I asked her if she minded him dressing like a woman.

She looked at me, stopped talking, and took a deep breath. "Of course I mind that. I guess I've been too focused on my clothes being gone. I should look at the bigger problem. I don't want to be married to a cross-dresser."

Geraldine had other issues of her own to deal with that I won't elaborate here. But she was motivated to change and focused on her own childhood issues one at a time to gain insight and understanding of herself.

She shuddered as she talked, not sure if she could stay in her marriage anymore. As we discussed her dilemma, she decided that she would confront her husband. If he was willing to seek therapy to stop the cross-dressing, she might consider staying in the marriage. If he wouldn't, they were through.

She wanted to challenge him, but she didn't think she could. She wasn't used to doing that. Her quiet demeanor had allowed him to dominate the relationship. She always gave him his way. How could she change that now?

It took several weeks for her to think about what she would say when she talked to him. We role-played the conversation several times, and finally she was ready to give him an ultimatum.

Geraldine's husband told her he could get rid of his addiction, as he called it, by himself. He didn't think he needed a therapist. She agreed to let him try for two weeks.

At first, he succeeded. He stayed away from her undergarments and dresses for several days, but one day she found her things missing again and knew he was out with his friends.

Geraldine didn't know what to do. He hadn't listened to her, and now she was afraid to leave. She decided to deliver the ultimatum one more time. If he hadn't found a therapist by the end of the week, she would move out, taking her clothes with her.

He found a therapist the next day.

Geraldine shared her husband's story with me. When he was little, he thought his mother had all the fun. She had money and went to parties, making him stay home and babysit his little brother every night. Even though he'd tried his hardest to please her, she was always critical, and her husband never felt good enough. His mother isolated him from kids his own age. He could never go out with the other boys. He watched the girls at school going to parties and having fun—just like his mother. He was certain from a young age that girls were happier than boys.

Even though she was afraid, Geraldine told her husband that though she sympathized with him, she didn't want to live this way anymore. He made progress in therapy. He quit cross-dressing and going to parties. He joined a local golf association and played with several men in the neighborhood. He asked Geraldine if she wanted to golf too, and though she wasn't really interested in golf, she went because she wanted to save her marriage. The more she played, the better she liked it.

As her therapy progressed, Geraldine could see herself becoming more assertive. She joined Toastmasters International to improve her speaking ability. Little by little, she gained confidence in working with other people. She gave a presentation for a book club she belonged to.

Her beliefs about herself began to change. She wrote some mantras to remind her of her newfound perspective:

- Women can be assertive. I am assertive.
- I can share my feelings in my relationship.
- I have value in my relationship.
- I can share my thoughts and ideas with others.
- Others value my feelings.

Geraldine continued to become more outgoing. She loved her new life and the blessings this trial afforded her. She told me as she finished therapy that she felt like a flower coming into bloom and wished she had started sooner.

I suggested that she would appreciate it much more now than she would have earlier.

> "The rose and the thorn and sorrow and gladness are linked together."
>
> Saadi

Early Life Decisions

Growing up, June wanted a problem-free life. When she fell in love with a handsome young man who was kind and hardworking, she knew she was headed for a "happily ever after" type of life. She and her boyfriend married and had a family, but as the years went by, June could sense that something was wrong in her relationship. Her husband began to work late many nights. When she asked him about it, he told her he had extra jobs to finish before the end of the month. But the extra jobs were never-ending.

June did some investigating and found that he had had a pornography addiction since college. June called her best friend and cried. She shut herself away in her room. Her friend told her to divorce him.

What had happened to the problem-free life she'd thought she was getting? They had been together for twenty-five years. There were the children to consider.

At this point she could have beaten herself up for her choices:
- "Why did I marry him in the first place?"
- "Why wasn't I looking for this?"
- "I am so blind!"
- "I feel like such a fool!"

Instead, her pastor encouraged both her and her husband to seek therapy. Her husband agreed to counseling. *Both* of them worked hard in therapy. He attended an addiction group and participated in a rehabilitation program as well as separate sessions with his own therapist.

When I first saw June, she was depressed and overwhelmed with her situation. Laundry piled up and the house was a mess. She addressed her feelings of betrayal and anger by talking through them in therapy and journaling her thoughts. The couple learned to communicate on a deeper level than they ever had before. Slowly she recovered her ability to participate in daily life.

June and her husband came for couple's therapy. They learned to be more honest and open with each other. Their friendship grew as they nurtured the relationship. When a problem came up, June addressed it instead of feeling helpless and afraid.

As she finished therapy, I asked June if she thought she had made a mistake in marrying her husband. She said when she first found out about the pornography, she would have said yes, but now she could see all the good that had come from their troubles. She gained a lot of strength from her trial.

The Rewards

Each problem we encounter and overcome will give us remuneration. The greatest times of individual growth come from addressing a crisis and embracing the blessings it gives us. Be solution focused to resolve the difficulty in the best way possible. Remember that there is no "right" or "wrong" way. Everyone does things differently, and the important thing is doing what seems right for you.

Decide what you will do differently next time. Explore all the options but be gentle with yourself. Don't beat yourself up and tell yourself you are "stupid" or any other destructive things you are in the habit of calling yourself. Use your positive affirmations and gratitude statements. Look at your trials and problems as learning experiences. Difficulties are inevitable, but the way we look at them is our choice. We can choose to be in a state of despair, or we can opt for a solution-focused attitude. Stay positive so optimistic energy can surround you. Look to your higher power for blessings.

> "A vision without a task is but a dream, a task without a vision is drudgery, a vision with a task is the hope of the world."
>
> Unknown

Create your vision and find the tasks that will make your dream possible. Ask your family and friends to support you.

The small caterpillar is breathing in the fresh air of life through the holes in the side of her body called spiracles. She knows that life isn't perfect, but she clings to her branch and continues to munch her way through every day. Her skin is growing too small—changes are coming too fast for her outer covering to keep up.

You are also recreating yourself, one day at a time. You struggle and advance, enlarging your soul, able to face the challenges of life in a timely fashion with success and a feeling of peace.

Intrinsic Gladness Is the Passport to Triumph

Overview Steps:

- Define the challenge
- Seek the advice of a wise teacher:
    - Religious leader
    - Trusted friend
    - Mentor
- List long-term goals to overcome your challenge
- Define short-term steps
- Begin your plan of action
- Follow through
- Continue to seek wisdom from your teacher
- Use positive affirmations
- Make gratitude talk part of your daily ritual
- Be positive in all you do
- Visualize positive energy around you

Chapter 6

Healing Fear

I do not want to be crippled by fear.

Fear is the basic underlying cause of many subjects discussed in this book. As you read each chapter, look at your specific difficulties. Keep fear in mind as at least part of the cause. **Fear can be defined as false expectations appearing real.** If you can see fear in the light of false expectations, it is plausible to talk yourself out of it. Use positive "self-talk" to take away the emotionality associated with your fear. Remember, it takes time to change a habit, so encourage yourself over and over again.

> "For God hath not given us the spirit of fear, but of power, and of love, and of a sound mind."
>
> *2 Timothy 1:7*

Childhood Fears

As a child I was afraid of the dark. I heard stories about beds falling through the floor and the Boogie Man. I remember seeing the Wizard of Oz and having bad dreams for weeks after. My husband also had childhood fears. He used to throw his shoes under the bed each night—hard enough to make the monster yell, if it were really there.

As we grow up, we tuck those childhood fears away. We know the bedroom floor won't fall in, and that there are no monsters under the bed.

But we hang on to the fear. It takes on a more sophisticated nature, such as fear of making friends with new people, fear of germs, fear of having and trusting your dreams, or fear of moving forward with goals you want to achieve.

Overcoming Fear

How do we overcome these fears? It's healing for us to help the child inside of us let go of old fears. When we comfort that small child within us, part of us is made whole. As past fears heal, present day ones are less difficult to work through.

Create a healing visualization of you, the adult, comforting you, the fearful child. I can picture the little child I was, in red flannel pajamas, going to bed. My present-day self holds her and loves her. I tell the little girl in red that I will keep her safe and protect her. She and I find a nightlight, or turn on the hall light in our visualization. We are able to bolster the floor so it will stand strong. I comfort and love her.

She and I talk about all the positives concerning the dark: the beauty of the moon and stars, the friendly sounds of the crickets or the soothing hoot of an owl, the smell of night air, the touch of the cool sheets when climbing into bed. When I comfort her, I feel better also. If "who we are" mentors "who we were," healing takes place. I love the night now because it's peaceful and restful.

Let's look at a more sophisticated example. How about the fear of making friends? Can you find the outgoing nature inside of yourself? Can you visualize yourself enjoying the company of someone new? Take a sincere interest in others and learn about them. Give back to mankind as mankind has given to you. Be empathetic and kind.

As a teen, my family moved to a new city. I was invited to a social tea for the most popular high school girls in town. Intimidation washed over me. I didn't want to go, but my mother kept telling me I had to. When I got there, no one came up to talk to me. After I said hello to a few people, I left. As I look back on the situation, there were other girls standing around waiting for someone to talk to them as well. I could have visited with them, but my fear was too great. I have skills and maturity now that

I didn't have then. I am sincerely interested in new people. I want to learn about others and be with them. In this frame of mind I take pleasure in greeting and listening to those around me.

Debilitating Fears

Debilitating fears can alter your lifestyle. If your worry about germs causes you to wash your hands excessively or clean compulsively, it is keeping you from the joys and blessings of positive energy. I worked with a dear lady, Della, who was bound by ritualistic behavior concerning, among other things, her household cleaning. The bathroom sink had to be scrubbed clockwise and tapped in several places in order to be sanitary. Della feared illness if she wasn't precise in her ritual.

A psychiatrist helped with her medications, and she addressed her behaviors in therapy. As a child her father abused her, and her mother was a meticulous housekeeper, constantly warning Della that she would get sick if she didn't do even the smallest things.

In counseling Della learned to soothe herself through positive self-talk. Several of the affirmations she wrote herself were
- My body is strong and healthy.
- I can clean my sink in any way I wish.
- I can let go of fear. It doesn't serve me well.
- My internal strength comes from inner wisdom.
- I am a creation of infinite worth.

She developed an extensive set of affirmations and said them to herself several times a day. She listened to soft music of her choice when her palms began to sweat and she found herself pacing the floor with nervous energy. Visualizing herself as a whole, healthy person helped her let go of the rituals a little at a time. She came to know that the bathroom sink would be sanitary no matter which direction she scrubbed it, and that she didn't need to tap the mail six times on each corner before she opened it. Progress was slow, but she walked the healing path.

"*The whole secret of existence is to have no fear.*"

Buddha

Systematic Desensitization

Another client, Betty, feared small, enclosed spaces, like elevators. She and I worked together using systematic desensitization, which means making yourself less nervous about a situation or an object through gradual exposure. You face your fear one step at a time. Betty used affirmative self-talk as she practiced the following:

Step 1: Walk into the elevator and walk out again. Repeat this step until anxiety has lessened. As Betty performed this task, she used positive statements to encourage herself. She also visualized herself completing this goal.

Step 2: Walk into the elevator and close the door. Open it immediately and walk out. Betty repeated this step until her uneasiness diminished. While she worked, she practiced breathing slowly and steadily and said her affirmations.

Step 3: Walk into the elevator, close the door, and ride up one floor. Open the door and immediately get out. As Betty rode the elevator over and over, her anxiety and fear lessened. She felt a great victory. She could check into a hotel and not worry about getting to her room.

The steps got increasingly difficult, until she could ride the elevator to the floor of her choice.

She addressed other anxieties as well—such as small hallways, closets, and little bathrooms. She desensitized herself to those through similar steps as the ones she took with the elevator.

However, she never put herself into close crowded spaces unless it was necessary. You wouldn't find her in New York's Time Square on New Year's Eve or running onto the football field to join the masses in a victory celebration. She didn't, and still doesn't, care to have those types of experiences. Betty learned to live a life that was comfortable for her.

"Always do what you are afraid to do."
Ralph Waldo Emerson

It is important to have a coach or a friend with you at all times as you practice the steps. If panic attacks accompany your anxiety, be sure to seek psychiatric help along with therapy.

Use this same pattern for any specific fear. Look for the positives concerning your problem. Allow yourself to replace anxiety with internal light and peace.

The growing caterpillar has fears of being eaten but knows her body is offensive to many predators because of the poisonous milkweed she's eaten. She feels the protecting hand of creation and is at peace.

You, likewise, are in the process of letting go of your fears. You feel the presence of the persevering love of your higher power and find unity with life.

Private Serenity Is Vital to Self-Actualization

Overview Steps:

- Journal the problem
- Set a goal
- Visualize and comfort the child you were
- Listen to the fears of the child that you were
- Rewrite childhood fears with visualization
- Reassure the child
- Fix the problems for the child
- Look for the positives of a fearful situation
- Step into fearful situations by
  - Taking a deep breath
  - Using positive affirmations to assert your value as a person
  - Feeling your inner strength
  - Sharing your goodness with others
- If debilitating fears exist
  - Find a psychiatrist for medication
  - Find a coach or therapist
  - Use systematic desensitization
- Set a program that works for you, e.g.
  - Positive self-talk
  - Music
  - Positive visualization
- Visualize the presence of peace and light and let its energy envelop you.

Chapter 7

Finding Personal Power

I do not want to be afraid to be by myself.

Love of Self

If I can't take pleasure in my own company, I can't receive the goodness others send my way. If I am comfortable with myself, I can accept outside love.

> *"Love thy neighbor as thyself."*
>
> *Mark 12:31*

> *"You yourself, as much as anybody in the entire universe, deserve your love and affection."*
>
> *Buddha*

Self-nurturing and love is the basis for all our relationships. If we do not love ourselves, we cannot love our neighbor.

When we discuss self-love, a label of narcissism comes to mind. Enjoying time by yourself and developing feelings of self-worth are very different from narcissism, which can be defined as vanity, selfishness, egotism. Narcissistic people feel like they are entitled to privileges and deference from others. They do not care for self or others in a nurturing way.

Being Alone

Joan hated being alone. She made sure someone was with her at all times. She panicked when she was by herself and escaped immediately into a television movie.

She came to therapy to work through this fear. As a child she remembered feeling useless and unlovable. As an adult she involved herself in fast, intense relationships with men, wanting them to heal her negative self-image. She clung to them, calling them often during the day and needing to be with them as soon as they were off work. These relationships never lasted. Her friendships with other women followed the same pattern.

If someone acted differently than she thought they should, she felt discarded and told them so. If her boyfriend didn't call when she thought he should, she would get angry. If an acquaintance at the office didn't ask her to go out for lunch, she was offended. When friendships ended because of her anger, Joan felt rejected and worthless. She kept recreating situations that reinforced her insecurities—her childhood wounds. Joan asked others for something only she could provide for herself.

When we look to others to fill our unmet needs, it is never enough.

Joan was a very intelligent and insightful person. She knew she needed to change her pattern of interaction with people, but first she needed to become comfortable with herself.

Joan began by writing positive affirmations for herself:

- I love myself.
- I care about myself.
- I enjoy my own company.
- I like to hang out with myself.
- I am a good friend to myself.

Joan made a list of things she could do by herself, such as reading, listening to music, and giving service. Since she wanted to re-parent herself, she decided to start by reading children's books. She set a goal to read the entire list of Newbery Medal Books (the American Library Association's award for outstanding children's novels). Christopher Paul Curtis's *Bud, Not Buddy* made her laugh. She loved how the characters in Avi's *Crispin: The Cross of Lead* and Linda Sue Park's *A Single Shard* gained internal strength as the stories unfolded. Karen Hesse's *Out of the Dust*, Cynthia Rylant's *Missing May*, and Cynthia Voigt's *Dicey's Song* were among her favorites. The pattern for her own personal power defined itself from the literature she read.

Listening to music inspired Joan. She downloaded specific pieces that she enjoyed and found relaxing.

She helped an elderly neighbor by reading to her in the evenings. This lady loved Joan and relied on her company.

Joan learned to be grateful for each moment. She enjoyed the bright sun on the red mountains of the desert around her and marveled at the electronic devices she had in her kitchen to aid her meal preparation. She started to take pleasure in having time to be alone—to feel secure in her own company.

The greatest gift Joan received in this process was the reward of self-awareness. She began to dream her dreams and expand her goals. She is cautious in friendships, but is starting to develop longer-lasting relationships with both men and women.

Positive Self-Talk

Vera had difficulty making decisions. She relied on her friend Mary to help her. Mary got engaged, and Vera worried about Mary leaving her. She had always had Mary to help her with everything, and she didn't know how to make a decision on her own.

Her first assignment when she started coming to me was to find out all the information she could about a subject. She listed the pros and cons on a sheet of paper. Then she gave herself time to think about what would be best for her.

She learned the decision-making process, but when she finally reached a conclusion, she immediately second-guessed it. She was critical of herself, often dismissing her feelings and decisions.

The next assignment Vera undertook was to write positive statements about her decision-making progress. When she used this positive self-talk, she could see that she'd made a good choice, but she had a hard time quieting her negative self-talk and internal feelings.

I asked Vera to list the positives she saw in herself. She couldn't think of any, so we created a new strategy.

It's difficult to be as kind to ourselves as we are to others. Vera trusted Mary in a way she could not trust herself, even though the two women were alike in many ways. Vera possessed a lot of the same characteristics as Mary, such as her ability to empathize with others and her capacity for hard work. She couldn't figure out why she wasn't able to relate to herself in the same positive way she did with Mary.

Vera made a list of all the things she liked about Mary. Then she circled the items that were similar to her own attributes. Then Mary went over the list with her and found a few more.

Vera selected three characteristics from the list that she believed she could improve in herself:
- Listen to herself
- Accept her own ideas when making a decision
- Use positive self-talk

She set a goal to do one thing on the list each day, like listening to herself or saying something positive about herself. She felt like she had mastered each after two weeks, so she chose three more items from the list for the following weeks. After six weeks, she could see her worth and felt better about herself. She began to sense her internal power. She set new goals, confident that she could achieve them.

Vera told others about her goals and started to use a memory jogger to keep herself on track. She put a penny in her shoe to remind her to listen and be kind to herself. Vera had a friend at work who decided to use his own memory jogger. He put a penny in his shoe every time he said something negative about himself. Soon his shoe became so heavy he couldn't walk.

If you focus on the negative, it begins to imprison you like the cocoon of the caterpillar.

A candy junky from Vera's work used jellybeans as a memory jogger. He started with ten each morning. If he was positive with himself, he got to eat the jellybeans with lunch. Every time he was critical of himself, he had to give a jellybean away to a friend. He soon learned to be positive because he wanted that candy for himself.

Surrounded by friends and supporters, including herself, Vera came to know her own mind and rely on her own judgment.

> "You can't just sit there and wait for people to give you that golden dream. You've got to get out there and make it happen for yourself."
>
> Diana Ross

Body Image

The overwhelming majority of the women I worked with had a poor body image. One client thought her nose was ugly. Another said her ankles were thick. Thin teens saw themselves as fat.

You are not your body. You are so much more than just your physical body.

A client, Mandy, had a kind, gentle personality. She was a good mother, gave service in her community, and loved her neighbors. However, Mandy thought she was ugly and fat. (She wore a size 14 dress.) It didn't matter how much others praised her. The words they said were like water running off a duck's back. Until she was able to care for herself, she couldn't let the praises in.

The only way Mandy was able to motivate herself to change was to see that she was teaching her daughter negative self-talk and body image. She wanted her daughter to feel good about herself, so she set up and then began carrying out some positive assignments for herself so that she could feel that way too.

> "It's pretty hard to start a child out in the way he should go if that isn't the way you are going."
>
> Unknown

Mandy got a haircut and a manicure. She began to nurture herself by rubbing her hands and her feet with lotion once a day. Her body image was so negative that this was a difficult task for her. As soon as she felt comfortable with that, she went on to lotion her lower legs and lower arms. Each week she included another part of her body. It was a slow process of change for Mandy, but she was happy with her progress.

It is difficult to alter lifelong habits of thinking and behaving. It doesn't happen overnight. It takes motivation. Mandy is beginning to know she is so much more than just her body. She is full of love and beauty and power.

Focus on Others

It is interesting to note that both Vera and Mandy began their healing process by focusing on someone else. Vera focused on her friend's attributes before she could see the good in herself. Mandy began her healing process for her daughter, not herself.

Explore the characteristics of people you enjoy being around. List their qualities. How many do you possess? Get feedback from a reliable friend—someone who will not just appease you, but will honestly tell you the good things about yourself. Now make a list of your own qualities. The inventory will grow as you really get serious about who you are.

Remember that birds of a feather flock together. We tend to choose friends who are similar to ourselves. You will probably find that you have many of the same good qualities as your friends.

Maybe there are some traits that you want to possess but don't. How can you begin to develop them?

Define a new, positive characteristic about yourself. Share your idea with a friend. Practice it until it becomes a habit. Feel gratitude for your newfound strength.

For instance, if you want to be more sensitive to others, what kind of strategies can you incorporate in your program?

- Visualize yourself listening more effectively.
- Send a small note of thanks to someone for a job well done.
- Write a text message to boost someone's morale.
- Set several small goals that you can achieve each day.

Focus on your positives! Be grateful for who you are and what you are. Gratitude is a powerful healing tool. Use it daily. If I begin each day with gratitude, I am happy the entire day. Thankfulness will take you into affirmative energy in a soul-expanding way.

Attract the Positive

We attract the things we think about and believe. Look to a wise teacher for help. What are their teachings about believing in yourself?

"If thou canst believe, all things are possible to him that believeth."
Mark 9:23

Use this statement, or find similar statements in your chosen belief system.

Our tiny caterpillar has outgrown her protective skin once, twice, and now for the third time. She continues to grow and change, becoming more than she ever thought she could be as she surges toward her goal of becoming free.

You are also accessing the positive energy around you as you set your goals and believe in yourself. Your dreams are becoming a reality and your vision is close enough to touch.

Felicity Is the Key to Wholeness

Overview Steps:

- Learn about yourself
  - Journal
  - Have a conversation with yourself.
    - Listen to yourself.
    - Identify your fears?
    - Let them go.
- List the attributes of a good friend.
  - Count how many of these attributes you already have
  - Identify the ones you want to develop
  - Have the friend review your list
  - Focus on several characteristics you want to become comfortable with
  - Compliment yourself on the ones you exhibit.
  - Remember that you are infinitely more than your body
  - Pamper yourself
  - Systematically desensitize yourself to negative body image
- Share your goals with a friend
  - Work together
  - Add new attributes to your goals
- Remember that gratitude brings positive energy
- Believe in yourself
- Set goals
- Dream dreams

Chapter 8

Decision Making: Releasing Confusion

I cannot make up my mind—I feel confused.

Many people allow confusion to irritate their lives and bring them negative energy.

I have a friend who asked me to meet her at the airport when she came home from a trip to Florida. She had golf clubs and luggage to pick up. I agreed to wait for her at arrivals. She sent me a text, changing her mind and wanting me to be at the drop-off for departures because it was a shorter distance to carry her baggage. Then she changed her mind back to arrivals. By the time we finished the text, I didn't know where to pick her up. I asked her one more time where she wanted me to meet her, and she told me arrivals. When I got to the airport and went to arrivals, she wasn't there. I found her at departures.

Confusion Creates Crisis

We can complicate things by changing a decision back and forth. What's the payoff for this type of behavior? Why do people do it?

This thought pattern keeps one in a state of crisis, never knowing exactly what's going to happen. There is an element of confusion that goes with this thinking. It also keeps unfavorable energy flowing. It keeps you imprisoned so you cannot access the positive energy around you.

> "It is our choices, Harry, that show what we truly are, far more than our abilities."
>
> J.K. Rowling

People who are black-and-white thinkers tend to vacillate when making a decision because they worry about being wrong. The truth is, most decisions are neither right nor wrong. If a group of people were asked to make individual choices, many varied answers would be given. Decide what's best for you and follow your dream.

Insecurity Causes Hesitancy

There are many reasons for hesitation in the decision-making process, but fear and insecurity head the list. You may feel inadequate making choices. You might say your choices have not been very good in the past.

I say, stop looking at the negatives. You have also made some good choices. Focus on them. Even though some of my choices were not the best, they have turned into great teaching moments for me. I have learned more from them than I have from my good choices.

Madison came from an alcoholic family. Her parents were divorced, and no one took time to help her learn how to make wise decisions.

Madison got into credit card debt as a teen and didn't know how to get out. As she began to look for solutions, she found a support group with Debtors Anonymous. She learned helpful skills from the people there and became better at managing her money.

Rather than continue to focus on her youthful, irresponsible decisions, she looked at the present positive choices she made. She was grateful for the lessons she learned from her poor selections. The more she focused on the constructive skills she learned, the more she trusted herself.

A Need to Please Others Causes Uncertainty

Some people have a hard time making a decision because they want to please everyone. They sit on the fence and are afraid to get off on one side or the other.

Chloe came from a family of physicists: her grandfather, mother and brother all worked in the Physics Department at a nearby university.

Chloe loved art and wanted to pursue a career in interior design, but she was afraid to tell her mother because Chloe knew she would disapprove.

Chloe registered for interior design classes at the university without letting her mother know. She usually told her mother everything, so she felt guilty going behind her mother's back—besides, everyone at the school knew her mother, and someone was sure to tell. Chloe shared her problem with her professor, and he advised her to be honest. He knew her mother and suspected that she would "bluster at first, but then she'll calm down."

Chloe was scared, but she decided to follow her teacher's suggestion. When she told her mother, Chloe got the "lecture of her life." She went to bed that night unable to sleep, feeling terrible. How could she follow her dreams and still get along with her mother?

The next day her mother peeked in Chloe's bedroom door and thanked Chloe for being honest. Her mother said she would try to understand, but interior design was not "her thing." They both listened to each other and agreed to disagree. Relief flooded through Chloe. Being honest had been the best choice. Now she could share her excitement about her career with everyone.

The Decision-Making Process

> *"Good decisions come from experience, and experience comes from bad decisions."*
>
> Unknown

What if you don't know what you want? There are times when I fall into this category. I have to think about certain decisions for a while. If I list the pros and cons and give myself a little latitude, I can usually find what works for me, but it takes me some time.

Look at the past to see what your decision-making pattern has been. Then assess your present situation in the context of the past. This process will work only if you have a positive outlook. If your view is negative, you will stay stuck in a downward cycle. You have to stay positive for this evaluation process to work.

If indecisiveness is part of your thinking pattern, look for the behavior payoffs. If you find yourself slipping into black-and-white thinking, or if fear and insecurity plague you, tell yourself to stop and change your thinking to the positive.

- Brainstorm all possible solutions.
- Consider each idea separately.
- Study the pros and cons of each.
- Choose the best idea for you.

This may seem tedious at first, but it's a good way to change your thinking pattern and become a solution-focused person. The following are a few of many ways to complete this process:

- Make a list on a piece of paper.
- Journal your thoughts.
- Have a discussion in your head. Represent both pros and cons.
- Talk out loud while looking in the mirror.
- Discuss the process with a loved one or a friend.
- Make a decision and stick to it.

Celebrate your goodness and your power. Know that you have the internal strength to make great decisions. This is a powerful tool to keep optimistic energy in the forefront of your life. Blessings will flow to you.

Strength and confidence envelop our caterpillar. Metamorphosis is almost complete. She molts a fourth time. When flies and other insects bother her, she flicks them away with her antennae. Things that would have upset her in the past are now no more than a swipe with her feelers.

You, likewise, are modifying yourself and swelling with the success of releasing confusion and moving forward with life. The exhilaration of accomplishment and positive energy is yours.

Self-Trust Is the Key to Achievement

Overview Steps:

- Journal times of indecision
- Look for patterns
- Figure out what your payoff is for the behavior:
  - Crisis
  - Confusion
  - Flow of negative energy
- Use thought stopping
- Brainstorm solutions
- List pros and cons of each option
- Become solution focused
- Have a discussion in your head
- Talk to yourself in the mirror
- Fill your life with the positive concerning your choices
- Add gratitude and blessing to the decisions you make

Chapter 9

Decision Making: Self-Trust

I do not want to rely on others to make my decisions.

Developmental Decisions

Decision making is a process that begins in childhood. If a child learns to make simple decisions when she's young, like choosing her clothes, she will develop a solution-focused pattern of thinking that will aid her later in life. Allow a child to make as many decisions as possible. Let her choose her own books at the library, the kind of vegetables she wants at the grocery store, the type of sandwich she will eat for lunch, and the game she wants to play. Every decision she makes will build her self-esteem, especially if she knows she has a caring adult who values her opinion. If you have questions on this subject, find a parenting guide that will fit your needs. There are many excellent books available.

Wanda's three-year-old daughter, Sophie, loved to try on dress-up clothes. Wanda gave her daughter a whole drawer of play clothes she could change into as many times a day as she wished. However, Sophie knew that on preschool days, she couldn't wear dress-ups. She had school outfits to pick from. (This pattern worked for Wanda, but I know some mothers that don't care if their children wear dress-ups to preschool. Find the way that's best for you).

Elizabeth's son Jeffrey loved Legos. He spent hours building towers and cars and airplanes, searching for just the piece he needed for a certain design he was creating. Sometimes Elizabeth would help Jeffrey find the specific blocks he needed to complete a project. This play entailed a lot of decision making, which Elizabeth reinforced by validating Jeffrey's choices.

A child picks up on our communication patterns. If you are indecisive, your child will learn your hesitation. If you model good decision making, your children will follow suit.

Sunday morning used to be a disaster at Tami's house. Several of her teenage daughters couldn't make up their minds about what to wear to church. They would each discuss the pros and cons of tens of outfits every Sunday. They listened to each other's advice, and then argued about every article of clothing. They would trade clothes and shoes, and then trade back again.

Tami allowed the girls to make their own decisions and didn't enter into the conflict. They were old enough to work things out for themselves. Tami confided to me that she thought she would go crazy before she got the girls raised.

Teens often share clothes with each other. It's a good way for them to decide what they really like and learn to make decisions. It's connecting time for them.

Self-actualization develops as you are able to define yourself in the context of relationships with others.

Tami's daughters have all grown into responsible women who know what they want and have learned the art of decision making—and Tami survived the process.

Young adults need time to explore and try different paths. That means choices in career, relationships, hobbies, and philosophical options. There is so much of the world to explore before their own inner wisdom guides them to a chosen course in life.

Major Decisions

There are major decisions to make. For instance:
- Which college to attend.
- What vocation to pursue.
- Whom to marry.
- What house to buy.

For big decisions, gather as much information as possible. Read all you can on the subject and ask the opinions of others. Study the situation thoroughly. Most importantly, take your time. In the process of making these decisions, you come to know yourself.

I had a client, Cary, in her late thirties who couldn't decide whether she wanted to get married or not. She found a kind man and fell deeply in love, but she had several friends with differing views on marriage giving her advice. One friend had just come out of an angry divorce and counseled Cary against marriage completely. She thought living together would be the best. Another friend was a romantic and told Cary that marriage meant happily-ever-after. A third friend told Cary she was past her prime and set in her ways and therefore shouldn't consider marriage because she would be unable to adapt to a new lifestyle.

In therapy, Cary explored the pros and cons of her decision and was able to choose for herself. She and her boyfriend read and talked about what they wanted and expected in a marriage. They found they had a lot in common.

Cary could see that her friends each viewed the world differently, according to their own experiences. It followed that she also had her own experiences and views on the world so she needed to decide for herself.

It's great to listen to those around you, but be sure to find the differences between your world and that of your associates. During this process, Cary learned to define herself in the context of her relationships with others.

> "Be willing to make decisions. That's the most important quality in a good leader."
>
> *General George Patton*

Daily Decisions

Relying on others for daily decisions invalidates you as a person. You can become stuck and unable to grow if you allow others to make your decisions for you.

Ella couldn't make up her mind about anything. Her husband chose her clothes in the morning. She let others decide where she would go for lunch. It took her months to decide on a new car because her father told her an SUV would be best, but her husband wanted her to get a sports car so he could drive it. At the grocery store she studied the shampoo aisle for thirty minutes, trying to decide which kind would be "right" for her.

Ella was depressed, helpless, and angry.

What was the payoff for allowing others to make her decisions? She didn't have to take responsibility for her actions. She could always blame someone else if things didn't turn out to her liking. She kept herself in a negative, helpless state of confusion.

Healing this type of negative behavior must start with self-trust and inner wisdom.

Self-Trust

Ella didn't learn to trust herself when she was young. A controlling mother and an absent father didn't foster Ella's self-esteem. She was into her forties before she came to really know and stand up for herself. It was a step-by-step process from then on.

About this same time, Ella began a degree in higher education. She had a great college professor who told her she wrote thoughtful papers. She could see Ella's wisdom, even though Ella couldn't. Ella began to listen when her professor told her she had valuable ideas. She let it soak into her being. When she broke through the imprisonment of self-doubt and let her professor's compliments in, she could let love in from other places as well. She had always known her husband cared about her, but now she began to let his love inside her. She began to say thank you to the people at her church when they complimented her.

As her self-confidence grew, Ella learned about herself—one decision at a time. She picked out her own clothes in the morning and found a shampoo she liked. With each choice, Ella trusted herself more and more.

> "Freedom, after all, is simply being able to live with the consequences of your decisions."
>
> James Mullen

As you become more proactive in your daily decisions, you will learn to trust yourself and feel confident in your judgment. You will come to know the things that you want and the things that will be best for you.

The Twenty-Four Hour Rule

When making a decision for myself, I listen to what others have to say. Then I have a twenty-four hour rule. I give myself time to let the ideas percolate inside of me for twenty-four hours before making a decision. I know that I'm not good at snap judgments. I need to take some time to think and ponder my choices.

If you are good at thinking quickly and making sound, spur-of-the-moment judgments, that's wonderful. Many people work that way—I just know that *I* don't. Instead of beating myself up because I can't make quick decisions, I give myself permission to sit with something for a while until I can really think it over and decide.

I discuss the pros and cons with myself and check out all possibilities. Next I let it filter through my brain for twenty-four hours. During that time I am able to come up with other ideas that I wouldn't have thought of if I had made a hasty decision. Then, armed with accurate information, I make my choice.

Inner Wisdom

If you can allow positive energy and peace inside you, you will be able to access your inner wisdom. Find a comfortable place to sit or lie down. Visualize the muscles of your body relaxing. Begin with your toes and work your way up your body through your ankles, legs, etc., until you reach the top of your head. Breathe deeply, allowing your mind to be aware of your relaxation.

Generate a safe place in your mind. It might be in a soft grassy area under a shady tree, or a comfortable white sofa in a beautiful room.

Now find an inner guide in this safe place. It might be a trusted person in your life or a religious leader you rely on. Let this person walk toward you. Greet this person and tell them you appreciate their visit. Picture yourself sitting down in your safe place with this mentor. Share your problem. Discuss the pros and cons. Allow your inner guide to share his or her wisdom on the subject. Then ask this trusted person what you should do.

This experience ought to feel free and peaceful, with no apprehension. If you are anxious, discontinue the process and try again later when you feel more at peace. This inner guide must be someone or something you trust and value.

Come to know your internal guide. Create the visualization often enough that you build a close relationship with this person or object. Listen to your inner wisdom. As you use the imagery process described above you will access your divinity.

After your daydream, journal your thoughts and review them often. Writing will help you pull more detail from this experience. Discuss the things you have learned with yourself. Ask an external friend or companion to listen while you share the things you have discovered.

As a therapist, I became the inner guide for some of my clients until they had enough confidence to connect with their own wisdom. I had a woman in therapy with me who moved out of state. Several years later, I saw her at a conference, and she said she was doing well. She said that whenever she had a problem, she would say to herself, "What insight would Christy want me to see from this?" or "How would Christy help me handle this?" She used me as her voice, but she was really the guide and decision maker for herself. She'd had the knowledge inside her all along.

Choosing

To make a choice, first define the question. List all of the possible solutions or outcomes. Gain as much knowledge about the question as possible by doing the research to find out about it, and ask those around you for their input. Narrow the list of solutions to several specific options that seem best for you. Then access your own wisdom through your inner guide and listen. Afterwards, journal the process and sit with these few solutions a while before you decide.

Our caterpillar grows in confidence. She spins a delicate silky substance to a branch where her cocoon will soon hang. She molts for the fifth and final time, creating a chrysalis to protect her final refinement. This time she has learned to trust herself and her process. Her goal of freedom is in sight.

You are also full of confidence now as you reach down into the depth of your soul to trust yourself to make good decisions to guide you toward the existence you have always dreamed of.

Internal Wisdom Accesses a Better You

Overview Steps:

- Define the question
- List all possible solutions
- Research the question thoroughly
- Ask others for feedback
- Listen to your inner wisdom
- Discuss the situation with yourself and your inner guide
- Narrow your list of solutions to the several that seem best
- Give yourself a day to think about it
- Make your decision

Chapter 10

Personal Honesty

I don't want to be dishonest with myself or in my relationships.

Sometimes people say to me, "I don't know what I want." Come to know who you are so you don't use this phrase as an excuse. Being honest with yourself means taking responsibility for your life.

At times people don't share their feelings because they think, "My partner won't listen." That's an excuse also. If you look inside, you will usually find that it's fear that stops you from sharing, not other people. Tell others how you feel. Let them know where you are coming from.

Be truthful with those around you, but most of all, be truthful with yourself.

Honesty in Relationships

If you are honest in your communication with others, they will know where they stand with you and you will be a safe person to be around. They won't have to guess. But not everyone is like this. Some people keep their feelings bottled up inside, allowing them to fester so others aren't aware of what's happening in the relationship.

Jolyn wanted a divorce. She and Hugo had been married for twenty-five years, but she didn't feel connected to him anymore. There was no closeness in their relationship. She had managed the house and raised their two boys practically by herself, and now she was still responsible for all the household tasks, even though they both worked.

Hugo was panicked. He couldn't figure out why Jolyn wanted to separate.

As the couple talked, Jolyn said she had felt unappreciated for years, and she had let that resentment build inside of her. The least Hugo could do was help with the dishes and the laundry.

Hugo said that he was more than willing to help, if Jolyn would just tell him what to do. Jolyn resented that stance. She didn't want to have to tell him what to do; she wanted the two of them to work together. Hugo was willing to do whatever it took to save his marriage.

I asked Jolyn what had happened in her life to give her the internal strength to ask for a change. She said that over the years she had been afraid her husband would leave her if she were honest. After all, her parents had divorced when she was young.

She had just recently completed a positive thinking class and found the confidence she needed to let go of her communication fears. The second reason she felt empowered to ask for change was that she had a full-time job as an interior designer, so she could support herself if she were alone. I asked her which of the reasons influenced her most in her decision. She said both were catalysts. She needed the internal courage, but she also needed to know she could take care of herself if Hugo wouldn't listen to her.

Jolyn thought Hugo wouldn't help her. Thinking like this leads to misunderstandings, fighting, and, at times, the disaster of divorce. It is much healthier to share your feelings and allow your partner to respond. Don't make a decision until you've tried. Jolyn learned that Hugo was completely willing to accept more responsibility at home. He just needed to know what her expectations were, and what she needed.

It took several weeks before Jolyn's perspective changed. She found that the deeper issue for her was partnership. She wanted someone to be her companion. She had been lonely in her relationship and wanted a change.

Jolyn and Hugo learned some communication skills in therapy. She began to share her feelings, and he really began to listen. As the couple talked, Jolyn found the closeness she wanted. They began to do things together like they had when they were dating: skiing, rock climbing, movies, and country dancing.

Jolyn said she felt like a schoolgirl again, only this time falling in love had a deeper meaning for her because she was able to share herself.

Love of self leads to love of others, and that love returns a hundred fold.

You may be the one who needs to share your feelings in your relationship, as was the case with Jolyn. But what if the circumstances are reversed? Maybe you feel like your partner isn't being honest or open with you. What can you do in that situation?

Lorraine came into therapy puzzled, because she could feel a distance in her relationship with her husband. He joined her in therapy and agreed to do all the assignments given to him, but things didn't improve. In fact, he wanted to move out. Lorraine was devastated, and she didn't know what she had done. His actions were unexplainable. When she asked him if he was having an affair, he told her that he just wanted some time to be alone.

Several weeks after he moved out, she followed him from work and found him living with another woman. She found out that he had been cheating on her for several months but hadn't been honest, even when she asked.

Once she knew the truth, she was able to move on.

Lorraine stayed in therapy long enough to grieve the loss of her marriage. As she looked at patterns in her previous marriages, she could see that she and her chosen partners moved in and out of relationships by having affairs. She'd had an affair when she was married to her first husband. He had divorced her, and she'd married the man she was involved with at the time. Her second husband then had an affair a few years later. After their divorce, Lorraine became involved with her third husband while he was still married. He left his wife to marry her. And now he had just had an affair. Each of her marriages had lasted only about four or five years, ending with one of the partners being unfaithful.

Lorraine wanted a permanent relationship with someone she could love long-term. (Her parents had been married for fifty years.) She began to date a widower who had lost his wife after twenty-five years of marriage. They fell in love, and she knew he would be loyal to her because he had been faithful in his first marriage.

Being able to see the pattern in her first three marriages gave her the knowledge she needed to choose a different path. She and her present husband are honest with each other. They can share their feelings, and they are happy.

"Honesty is the first chapter of the book of wisdom."
Thomas Jefferson

Keep Power in Your Relationships

Lack of honesty can take other forms too. You can give your power up to those around you by allowing them to choose for you.

Vanessa was married to a gentle man who dominated her life in subtle ways. My husband and I went to dinner with them one night. When Vanessa finished her meal, she folded her napkin in a rectangle and then once more into a square and set it beside her plate. Her husband patted her shoulder and gently picked up Vanessa's folded napkin, shook it out and refolded it into a triangle.

When we were alone, I asked her about the napkin incident. She said, "He's always doing little things like that for me. He thinks they are kindnesses, but they make me feel like I can't do things right." She wanted to say something to him, but she didn't want to override his kindness. I asked her what would happen if she told her husband she wanted to fold her own napkin. She shrugged her shoulders and said it wouldn't make any difference.

Vanessa didn't have to make her own decisions. They were made for her. She could choose to step out of this communication pattern if she reached inside to find her inner courage, but she did not.

Her husband was a very mild, sweet, gentle man. How could she argue with that? As time went by I watched her become increasingly indecisive and passive. Her husband did more and more of her thinking for her.

What would happen if Vanessa told her husband she felt controlled? Could she say, in her kind and calm way, that she wanted her napkin left folded the way she had it? Would he listen? We don't know the answer to these questions.

If Vanessa said something about how she felt, it would empower her and give her more confidence. She thought her husband wouldn't listen, but if she stood firm she would be heard. He is a kind man who would probably listen if she told him how she felt. She doesn't need to yell or show anger. Honesty would give her strength. Many individuals don't realize the power they have in their relationships.

When you are with another person, how do you feel if they just "go along" with what you want? I worry when I'm in that situation because I feel like I have to guess at the other person's feelings. It's better if they tell me what they want, and then we work together toward that. Couples need to balance each other by sharing decision-making responsibilities.

Honesty with self and others engenders confidence.

Honesty and Intimacy

Jolyn and Hugo developed a closer relationship because they learned to be honest with each other about their feelings. Lorraine felt better when she learned about her husband's affair. Even though the information was hurtful, she was glad to have it so she could move on with her life. Secrets in families keep us stuck. Vanessa was afraid to move closer to her husband. She preferred to leave the relationship as it was, keeping the distance that seemed comfortable for both of them.

Honesty draws others to us.

Take some time to look at your own fears and see if they keep you from being honest in your relationships. Clear communication takes time and careful introspection. If you state your feelings about something, it doesn't need to be confrontational.

For example:

- "I feel lonely when you stay late at the office because I have no one to talk to in the evening."

- "I'm exhausted because I've been at work all day. I need to rest a few minutes, then let's fix dinner together."
- "I feel ___ about ___ because ___."

Give Yourself Time to Think

Another reason people abdicate their honesty in decision making is because they don't think quickly and have difficulty making snap judgments. Usually people like this are fairly easygoing and have to take time to think in order to know what they really want.

Being honest in your relationships can extend to friends and colleagues outside of a marriage or partnership. Telling others how you feel at work or at a party can be uncomfortable too.

A group of girlfriends loved to go to lunch together once a month, and took turns deciding where they would eat. Everyone had a choice—until it came to Molly. She couldn't select a restaurant. The friends waited patiently, but someone else finally ended up choosing for her. It happened over and over until her best friend pulled her aside and suggested she get some counseling.

Over Molly's lifetime, she had continually given others the freedom to choose for her. She said she didn't care about a lot of things, and that it was easier to let others decide.

She learned that she was not being responsible for herself. She had allowed herself to be like a child, permitting others to make her decisions and, at times, blaming others for making her choices.

Correct Decisions

Black-and-white thinking can cause hesitation in decision making. Those who worry about being right or wrong have difficulty settling on a plan of action. They think in "what if" statements—usually negative—which are pointless, since none of us can predict the future.

If we were to ask a group of people to make a decision, we would probably get different answers from almost everyone. It's great that we have choices, and even more wonderful that we can learn from our choices.

Molly hesitated to make decisions because she was worried that she would make an incorrect choice. What if the restaurant didn't serve food her friends would like? She feared failure and didn't trust herself.

She found she needed time to explore her options. She wanted to decide for herself, but it took her a while to sort things out. Molly needed a day to study the ideas—to feel confident that she had looked at an issue and knew what she felt would be best. When she gave herself permission to let things simmer around inside her head like a good stew, she was so much happier. She decided the next time it was her turn to choose the place for the monthly friend's lunch, she would think about it for a few days before and make her decision ahead of time.

Molly was exhilarated the first time she suggested a place for lunch. It was difficult at first, but she loves it now.

Being honest with yourself can bring confidence and power to you and your relationships. Self-esteem improves as you come to know yourself. It's a wonderful blessing to share yourself with those around you. They learn about the intimate parts of you as you begin to understand yourself.

The caterpillar begins the final coating process—protecting herself from outside elements so that she can perform her final piece of creative magic. Becoming free.

Now that you are honest with yourself, you know your internal strength, you can enjoy it with others. Light and energy surround you like a cocoon, refining you into more than you thought you could be.

Internal Honesty Leads to External Happiness

Overview Steps:

- Journal your honesty-with-yourself for two weeks
- List your honest communication with others for two weeks
- Write about the reasons for your lack of honesty:
    - Fear of loss in relationships
    - Habit
    - Laziness
    - Desire to abdicate responsibility
    - Lack of self-trust
    - Not knowing what you want
    - Inability to make spur-of-the-moment decisions
- Address your fear:
    - Use positive self-talk
    - Change your behavior
    - Brainstorm solutions
    - Use the twenty-four hour rule
    - Cut list down to possible options
- Practice changing your pattern
- Feel the positive energy and power of your newfound freedom
- Give gratitude for the blessing of being able to make decisions

Chapter 11

Being Sufficient

I do not want to feel I am never good enough.

Have you ever been around someone who felt her life was never good enough? That there was always something lacking? I had a friend who constantly found something wrong with her life. She could have received the world on a silver platter and still felt a void in some way.

What about you? Do you feel like you are never good enough? Do you find the negative even in a positive situation?

See the Good in Others

A beautiful young teenage girl, Erin, came into therapy. She and her mother didn't get along. When her mother was invited to a session with Erin, she was critical of her daughter. She couldn't find anything nice to say about Erin.

I asked her to step out into the waiting room until she could say something positive about Erin. She never returned to the therapy session.

It's incredibly sad that this mother couldn't see the good in her lovely young daughter. What a heartrending situation. A beautiful budding young woman wanted the love of her mother, and it wasn't available for her. Erin's story isn't a happy one. She ran away from home when she turned eighteen to live with boyfriend after boyfriend. I have since lost track of her, but I can't think of her without sadness. I wish her well and send positive energy to her often through my thoughts.

A friend of mine worried about her adult daughter, Sue. She tried to do as much as she could for Sue because she loved her. She listened when Sue talked for hours without offering advice, but she told me that Sue just complained and was never grateful. When she went to visit, Sue blamed her for the way her life had turned out and the situation she was in.

This is a simplified, single-dynamic version of the complex problems in this family, and positive self-talk alone couldn't solve their troubles. But optimistic thinking was an important facet of the change that needed to be made.

The payoff for this kind of negative, needy attitude is thinking that you can blame others for your problems. Those with this mindset believe they are not responsible for their behavior or themselves.

Personal Responsibility

How can Erin and Sue find happiness?

They can begin by taking personal responsibility for their situations and themselves. These girls are a product of their families. Both of them can choose to stay stuck in the places they find themselves, or they can choose to change their circumstances. Erin receives little love, while Sue has plenty but doesn't let it in. Erin would soak up any love her mother had to give. Sue rejects the love her mother gives her. Both Erin and Sue need to take control of their own lives.

We have been given families as a precious gift. It's sad when we don't see the goodness in each other. Evaluate your relationship with your family to see if you can improve it. People like Erin's mother are unavailable, so Erin may need to find motherly love from an aunt, a neighbor, or a wise mentor. Sue can be honest with her mother and let her know how she feels. She and her mother can work together to let caring into their lives.

Be open to finding love and caring when it comes. Whether from a family member or a friend, give love and receive it.

Positive Energy

We all thrive when affirmative energy surrounds us. See the potential in yourself and those around you and you will grow. Nourish yourself and others with optimism, gratitude, love, and caring. Create a positive energy cycle in your life: give love and it will come back to you. Feel the love that comes to you and you will want to give more love.

"Only love can be divided endlessly and still not diminish."
Anne Morrow Lindbergh

Internal Positive Energy

Maybe the criticism doesn't come from others; it might come from inside you. Perhaps you don't feel like you've done your best so far—it doesn't matter. The important thing is that you take responsibility for being where you are at this point in your life. You're now ready to make positive choices and be kind to yourself.

Change the Negative Thinking Habit

Negative thinking is a habit we learn from those around us as we grow up, or maybe we develop it ourselves over the years. What's important is how we can change it: with thought stopping. I like to say "STOP" in my head because it interrupts the negative thinking pattern and allows me to substitute a positive in its place.

Sometimes I'm angry and don't feel like replacing my negative attitude. Gratitude is an emotional softener for me. I say "STOP" in my head and begin a gratitude list. In a few minutes I have enough positive energy running through me to feel optimistic.

Gratitude is the greatest tool I have when it comes to pulling myself out of unfavorable thinking. If I start a gratitude list, I can go on and on, and I feel wonderful when I'm through.

Be Grateful for the Miracles in Your Life

"There are only two ways to live your life. One is as though nothing is a miracle. The other is as though everything is a miracle."
Albert Einstein

Look for daily miracles in your life. As I sit here at my computer, I can find miracles all around me. The mountains out my window are coming alive with the green of spring. The first leaf buds are on the rose bushes. My computer is a miracle to me. I remember using a typewriter. If I made a mistake, I had to use Wite-Out or start all over again.

Look at your body. Your nails protect the ends of your fingers. Your hair grows to cover your head. Your teeth make it possible for you to eat. There is no camera and video device that can compare with the intricacy of your eyes. No hearing apparatus or audio invention that has the sophistication of the human ear. No mechanical pump that could ever begin to match the human heart.

You are a miracle.

Nothing can compare with your human spirit. It can soar with happiness or take you to the depths of despair. It all depends on your attitude. The choice is yours. Fill yourself with positive light.

Accept Yourself

You are sufficient—even wonderful. Become comfortable with that term. Open your heart to see your best self. If we treat ourselves as we are, we will stay that way. But if we see ourselves as we can become, we will develop our potential.

Love what you are becoming.

Look for the best in yourself. Be grateful for who you are. Look for ways to enhance peace and light in your life. Positive affirmations, uplifting music, gratitude, and blessings journals are all ways to begin to bring affirmative thinking into your life. Expand the positive energy flow to your circle of family and friends. Miracles will happen in your life.

"*He who knoweth his own self, knoweth God.*"

Muhammad

As you radiate positive energy, it will come back to you, returning even a hundredfold. Try it!

Our caterpillar is hidden from view now, in the process of re-creation. At this point in her growth, the chrysalis is a protection from outside forces and a place for her to mature and change from within. It has the added goodness of providing her with camouflage so she can keep herself safe.

You have taken care to fill yourself with positive energy and accept yourself and the small miracles in your life. You are wonderful.

Love of Self Leads to Love of Others

Overview Steps:

- Take responsibility for yourself
- Know you have created your life as it is now
- Let go of negative energy
    - Use thought stopping
    - Keep gratitude lists or a journal
    - Count your blessings
    - Look for miracles around you
    - Give positive energy to family, relationships, and friendships
    - Develop loving relationships, as they are available to you
- Picture yourself as you are. It is enough
- Picture yourself as you want to become
- Look for ways to enhance peace and light in your life:
    - Positive affirmations
    - Uplifting music
    - Gratitude lists or journal

Chapter 12

Becoming Positive

I do not want to be stuck in self-deprecating talk.

Negativity Distances Others

> "There is little difference in people, but that little difference makes a big difference. The little difference is attitude. The big difference is whether it is positive or negative."
>
> W. Clement Stone

When we put ourselves down, we isolate ourselves because we think we are not as good as everyone else and think others won't give us the time of day. This keeps us from connecting. The criticalness really has to do with the negative energy inside of us. It has nothing to do with the other person.

An elderly lady, May, came in for counseling. She had many problems and began to sort through her feelings of betrayal and abandonment from her family. She was also upset at one of her neighbors. There was a woman living down the street who May said was unfriendly and rude to her. However, May couldn't give me any specific examples of the neighbor's impoliteness, except that the neighbor had never returned her greetings when May spoke to her. Later that year, May fell and broke her leg. She needed help to get groceries for the first few weeks. Guess who helped her and even brought her to her counseling appointment? Her new best friend, the neighbor woman.

May was ashamed of her harsh judgment and realized her criticalness had nothing to do with the neighbor. May couldn't find peace as long as she filled herself with derogatory statements about others. She began to understand that when she was negative about someone else, it was really about herself.

May began to let go of her negative talk and look for the positives in people. As she did so, her self-esteem improved, and she felt better about herself and others.

We are all children of a higher power. Whether we live on the streets of India or in the frozen tundra of Iceland, we are all the same. We all have hopes and dreams and can only become our best if we are positive.

Negativity Causes Anxiety

When Mercedes first came into therapy, she was sure that she would get fired from her job. When I asked her reasons, Mercedes couldn't give any. She just knew she would soon be unemployed.

> *"Fear is that little darkroom where negatives are developed."*
> *Michael Pritchard*

Mercedes's boss emailed her, asking for a meeting the next Friday. Mercedes was nervous as she anticipated the conference, sure that it would be her termination interview. She began to look in the want ads of the newspaper for new jobs. She searched the Internet in a panic. I told her to do some deep breathing and think positive thoughts. She didn't even know what the boss wanted yet.

When the day of the meeting arrived, she left a message on my phone—said she was "sweating bullets."

She called me after the interview to tell me that she was to be given a commendation for a new program she had developed. There was a special luncheon in her honor the next day and a bonus for her work.

Mercedes had experienced a lot of unnecessary worry over the interview with her boss. She had spent years living in fear and anxiety, and she was tired of it. She could finally see that her way of viewing herself and the world was skewed.

Mercedes started to say positive things about herself. She began to work on thought stopping and thought substitution. Her life became less stressful and a lot easier to live.

Optimism Elevates Mood

Anna came into therapy feeling depressed. Negativity had surrounded her as she was growing up. Her older brothers had always teased and taunted her, so she felt worthless. As a young adult she had moved to the United States from Spain. She saw herself as "less than" others in her new country because she struggled with the language and customs.

As Anna kept a journal, she found a surprising amount of cynicism. For two weeks she logged her thinking patterns and wrote pages of pessimistic self-incrimination and disapproval from others.

Anna felt awkward and uncomfortable as she began the thought-stopping process. She replaced her negativity with positive affirmations. At first she said them, but she didn't believe them. They seemed stilted—like lies. But she continued to say the words even though she didn't accept them as true.

"You affect your subconscious mind by verbal repetition."
W. Clement Stone

The negativity in her head was so deeply entrenched that it was hard to get rid of it all. Even when she did stop her pessimism, she felt a void. She needed to find substitutes to put in her head.

Anna read religious works about love and peace. She listened to positive self-help tapes. She also thought about a comedy she had just watched or a good book she was reading. She listened to audio books and good music.

Soon it became easier for Anna to feel positive about herself. She started to know her worth. It was a gradual process of change. She came to feel warmth and caring for herself.

Since Anna was a religious person, she was open to seeing herself as a divine creation. She looked at her hands and thought of the intricate muscles and bones that worked together. She was grateful that she could work in her garden in the rich soil. The petals of her roses unfolded in many different shapes and colors, and they were all stunning. She said they were like her life. Once she got past her thorns, her attractiveness appeared. Her gratitude talk brought her peace and diminished her negativity further.

Anna felt she had been given a special blessing in overcoming her negativity. She said there were many gifts from it: she greatly appreciated the peace she felt because she had known real depression and pain.

The Gratitude Key

I believe true happiness can only come with positive self-talk that includes gratitude. Thankfulness is a key ingredient in all religions and in all paths of wisdom. Positive self-talk doesn't necessarily need to be gratitude talk, but gratitude talk is usually positive. Be sure to include both positive self-talk and gratitude talk in your daily thinking patterns. As you awaken to each new day, make gratitude the first thing you do.

In the darkness of her chrysalis, our caterpillar produces chemicals to break down her body into a liquid in order to regenerate herself fully into the beautiful creature of her dreams—the exquisite butterfly she saw when she was no more than an egg.

You, likewise, are becoming a positive being, filling yourself with light and love, modulating yourself to energize into the best person you can become.

Serenity Brings Peace

Overview Steps:

- Keep a thought journal
    - Log all negative thinking for two weeks
    - Use thought stopping
    - Use positive replacements
    - Repeat affirmations
- Read religious literature
- Listen to self-help tapes
- Listen to audio books
- Enjoy to good music
- Watch comedy shows
- Read good fiction
- Enjoy positive movies
- Think about the miracles of life
- Realize your divine Nature
- Feel positive self-regard by using
    - Positive gratitude talk
    - Positive self-talk
- Wake up every morning to thankfulness

Chapter 13

Allowing Imperfection in Life

I do not want to be a perfectionist.

Sometimes being a perfectionist is wonderful. If you are working on a scientific experiment that will change the world, a violin concerto to be performed in Carnegie Hall, or a new race car for the Indy 500, you will probably want perfect results.

Never Good Enough

My husband loves to do carpentry work, and do it perfectly. He built a deck on our daughter and son-in-law's home over ground broken up by large tree roots. Since the earth was so uneven, he had to measure every few inches to be sure he had the supports the right length to make the wood deck level. He drove us all nuts because he measured every support over and over until it was perfect. But now the deck is beautiful and level. Sometimes perfectionism is great!

However, usually perfectionists see themselves as flawed—they never feel good enough.

> "The art of being wise is knowing what to overlook."
> William James

A perfectionist is never satisfied. The insatiable never-good-enough attitude in a perfectionist separates him or her from the light and love of positive energy, when the very gifts he or she needs to heal are that light and love. As the perfectionist begins to access these offerings, he or she can find peace.

As you go about daily life, you will probably not be perfect. Don't let your unattainable standards drive those around you crazy. You'll also feel unhappy with yourself and others who don't live up to your standards. Positive energy will elude you.

> *"People throw away what they could have by insisting on perfection, which they cannot have, and looking for it where they will never find it."*
>
> *Edith Schaeffer*

Letting Go of Perfection

Marilee was a "perfect" housekeeper. Nothing was ever out of place. When she and her husband had dirty clothes, Marilee didn't wait until she had a full load of laundry. She washed them immediately. She picked up her husband's newspaper and put in the recycling bin the minute he was through with it.

Marilee's world shattered when their first child was born—babies are messy. Her son drooled when his teeth came in. He dumped his oatmeal on the floor. He put spaghetti in his ear.

Marilee had to lower her perfection standards—an incredibly frustrating process. She talked to friends who listened, and then told her about their children stomping in mud puddles and spilling honey on the carpet. With time and effort, she learned to let go.

Marilee found that relaxing was a moment-by-moment experience. Some days were better than others. As Marilee kept a journal, she could see that her mood influenced her need for perfection. A negative mood drove her to higher standards. Positive feelings helped her to be a little more easygoing.

Marilee used optimistic affirmations and gratitude talk daily. She took time for herself and connected with others. She knew that being a good mother was more important than being clean, so she persevered.

She included compromise. The living room and dining room in her home could be "perfect," and most of the time she could let go of her flawless housekeeping standards in the kitchen and family room. But if she had a day where she couldn't, she called a friend to vent her feelings until she felt better. She loved her son enough to work on relaxing and forming a bond with him.

Life is not perfect for anyone. Everyone has problems at one time or another. We can take these trials, find solutions, and then look for the gifts and blessings in them.

Learning a Little at a Time

Nora loved to draw. She illustrated the Sunday programs for her church and made posters for upcoming activities. But she really wanted to learn to paint china. She took a class but was never satisfied—always comparing her work to others. Not ever feeling good enough overwhelmed her, and she dropped out of the group, letting the need for perfection keep her from developing and enjoying her talent.

Nora realized that she had to change her perspective if she wanted to be happy. In therapy she began to address her childhood of shame and abuse. Youthful fears overwhelmed and paralyzed her. As she worked through these feelings, she learned to fill her life with light and love and re-parent herself through positive affirmations and visualizations.

She began to work with a china-painting artist individually, rather than in a group setting. Meeting with the teacher alone helped Nora let go of her comparison thinking.

Letting go of her comparison thinking was a challenge. It was an ingrained habit that she'd had since she was a child. At first it was difficult, but after a couple of weeks with her pocket notebook she began to notice the pattern. Each time she found herself comparing, she said "STOP" in her head. Then she found a substitute thought:

- I am grateful that others have this skill.
- I can enjoy the beauty others create.
- I am thankful for my talent.

- I bring beauty to the world with my painting.
- As I develop my abilities, I fill myself with light.

Nora's teacher was nurturing and kind, and Nora blossomed under her tutelage. Nora gives beautiful platters and bowls as holiday gifts to her friends now. Her life is full because she and her friends are able to enjoy her art.

She was wonderful for who she *was*, not for what she *did*. Several years ago John Bradshaw talked about becoming a "human being" rather than a "human doing." We would all do well to live by that wisdom.

As a young child learns to walk, her falls and stumbles are not mistakes. They are helpful in teaching her about depth perception, the balance of her body, the strength of her muscles, and many other more specific skills.

Periods of growth are not mistakes, but times of maturing. Being solution focused is a good habit to get into. You are a butterfly emerging from a cocoon: you struggle and practice and develop and change.

> *"Perfectionism is the enemy of creation."*
> John Updike

Our used-to-be caterpillar is recycling her own body into a new one—releasing the old and embracing the new. Her dream is almost within her grasp.

Learning a little at a time becomes your motto as you allow imperfection into your life. The new you is embracing optimism and it permeates your entire being. Flight and freedom is within your reach.

Internal Contentment Leads to Maturation

Overview Steps:

- Remember that no one is perfect
- Journal your mistaken childhood beliefs
- Reframe your beliefs to be
  - Positive
  - Solution focused
  - Realistic
- Find the gift in each problem
- Shed your fear
- Remember that each difficulty is a learning experience
- Remember that times of growth are times of maturing
- Share your process with others
- Know that you are enough
- Know that your life is enough
- Know that your family is enough

Chapter 14

Releasing Depression

I do not want to be depressed.

Depression is a maelstrom of pessimistic energy that blocks the gifts of life quicker than almost anything. Where does your depression come from? Is it in your genes, or did you learn the negative self-talk from your surroundings?

These questions go back to the old Nature vs. Nurture argument. On the Nature side, genetic depression is passed down through generations. A negative view of life has been part of a person since birth. On the nurture side, a person learns negative thinking and speaking patterns in early childhood. Those around you always see the negative side of life, you pick up those patterns.

Arguments on both sides of the fence have avid supporters, but after the debate, the cure is still the same. You have to be proactive to change depression.

Changing the brain chemistry is necessary to reduce and alleviate depression. Transformation may be done through medication, a combination of medication and optimistic self-talk, or positive thinking alone. The best path often needs professional intervention. Find the direction that works well for you.

Depression is anger focused inward.

Negative Thinking Patterns

Negative thinking patterns can become ingrained in you as a minute-by-minute habit. It is difficult to break this way of looking at the world. But the persistent person will accomplish it.

A good friend from college, Angel, grew up in a home with negative parental communication. She could find the worst-case scenario quicker than lightning—I used to tease her about it when we were in school. She just couldn't see the positive in anything. As the years went by, she struggled to maintain quality in her life. She became withdrawn and finally escaped into a drug addiction she couldn't shake.

Angel attended twelve-step groups, but they didn't seem to help. She moved to a new job in a new city, but that made no difference. None of the external "fixes" seemed to change her. She worried about losing her husband and family over her addiction. Her depression deepened because she could see no solution.

Her minister kept encouraging her to give service in the community. He told Angel that kindness toward others would help more than anything else she could do. Angel tried volunteering at several religious and community-based organizations. That didn't help. She quit each one after a few weeks.

Finally, when Angel was really down, she heard that volunteers were needed at the local women's prison in a religious capacity. She decided to try working there a couple of days a week, and found she really liked the women she worked with. Many of them were depressed as well. When they talked, Angel could understand their feelings because she felt the same way.

The prisoners were assigned a positive self-help program to complete. It seemed to make a difference in the other women's lives, so Angel decided to try it herself. The program "clicked" in Angel's head, and she began to use the skills involved in the course. She had been resistant to change for years, and now she could accept it.

Angel learned about taking personal responsibility for herself. She quit waiting for someone to rescue her and fix her problem. She knew now that external changes couldn't help until she began to make internal changes.

As she modified her perspective, she quit feeling sorry for herself and began to look at her blessings. Positive self-talk and gratitude talk became a daily ritual for her. She read books on positive thinking to keep an optimistic viewpoint.

Angel wasn't different overnight, but over time I could see a change in her. Her life became hopeful. When I asked her how the transformation started, she told me she had come to a point where she had bottomed out and could see no way to go but up.

Angel taught herself to be solution focused, one day at a time, one difficulty at a time. Her quality of life is now better because she was proactive enough to change.

Angel could have benefited from therapy, and the change could have come much earlier in her life, but she didn't ever really think therapy would help—she didn't believe she could change. Attitude has so much to do with our healing process. Angel wasn't able to believe until she was involved with women who were really down and out and saw the change in them. If they could change, so could she. As her attitude turned around, she began to believe she could change, and she did.

Being Proactive Brings Maturity

A child will have good self-esteem if she is told that she is wonderful, but that alone isn't enough. The young person must be taught to be proactive rather than reactive. She must learn to take action toward solving problems rather than just whining about them. The same is true with adults.

> *"It is common sense to take a method and try it. If it fails, admit it and try another. But above all, try something."*
> —*Franklin Delano Roosevelt*

Be Solution Focused

Many of the clients I worked with would put themselves in double binds so there was no solution. If they made a decision to go right, they looked at the negative consequences. If they thought about going left, they could see things turning out badly. We become depressed and angry if there seems to be no solution to a problem.

"Happiness... lies in the joy of achievement, in the thrill of creative effort."

Franklin Delano Roosevelt

Riley came into therapy feeling depressed. The company she worked for was in financial crisis, and she had been demoted two grade levels and given a pay cut. She didn't want to stay in her current position because it was beneath her skill level. Riley was afraid to look for a new job because she thought her work expertise was out of date. She had put herself in a double bind. She could stay where she was using less skill and getting less money, or she could look for a job with her outdated abilities, which might keep her from getting one. In her view, both were negative alternatives.

On my suggestion, Riley began to redirect her thinking. In the process she did a job search and found her skills very marketable. She looked for and found new employment with good pay. Riley changed her thinking by obtaining more information so she was able to solve her problem.

Depression Is No Friend of Physical Exercise

When we talk about depression, we get so focused on eradicating negative thinking skills that we forget the basics—simple exercise is sometimes the best cure.

Makayla, who had been haunted by depression most of her life, came into therapy because she was unemployed and depressed. When she finished college, she chose a career in sales and found it very rewarding. She loved her product and enjoyed meeting and getting to know people. However, during the economic downturn, sales in her company dried up so she had to look elsewhere to make a living. She hated the work she found, and called in sick more and more often, staying home to lie on the couch and do nothing.

In therapy, Makayla set some positive thinking goals and kept looking for work she thought she would find rewarding. Finally, the owner of a pest control business offered her a job. Makayla liked the owner but wasn't sure killing bugs and routing out rats was her thing.

She took the job on a temporary basis and was surprised at the hidden benefits she found. Her depression lifted. She said she dropped twenty pounds almost immediately because of the physical exercise the job entailed. Crawling around attics and spraying grounds required her to be active. She liked meeting the families on her route and enjoyed bringing the security of a pest-free environment to them, but she tells everyone that the exercise is what released the death grip depression had on her.

> "A bear, however hard he tries, grows tubby without exercise."
> A. A. Milne

Find a type of physical activity you enjoy, and do it regularly. I take pleasure in weeding my rose bed. A friend loves to window shop in the mall. By the time she's looked in all the stores, she's walked a couple of miles. (She lives in Phoenix, where it's too hot to exercise outside much of the year.) My husband loves to golf. Three times a week, he's on the course with his friends. We have two daughters that swim. A grandson enjoys Irish dancing. Several years ago we vacationed to Italy. There, everyone strolls the streets in the evening. What a great cultural pastime! What is your passion?

> "Our increasing lack of physical fitness is a menace to our security."
> John F. Kennedy

Before you exercise, be sure you've checked with your doctor. Set a reasonable goal. If you have a hard time getting motivated, include a partner in your plan. Meet a friend for a walk in the park or take a yoga class together. Begin with fifteen minutes several times a week.

Benefits of exercise:
- It will boost your self-esteem.
- It's a distraction from your worries.
- It can include social interaction.
- You'll gain confidence in your abilities.
- You'll feel healthier.
- You'll be healthier.

> "Those who do not find time for exercise will have to find time for illness."
> Proverb

Let's ignore negative thinking and replace it with fun, esteem-building activities—play! Laugh, love, and enjoy your friends.

Looking for Love

A young adult, Victoria, came into therapy. Depression fueled her eating disorder. Victoria's parents had been divorced for almost ten years. Her father remarried and had a second family. They lived in a small supportive community where the majority of the people were religious. The family seemed happy.

Victoria wanted that kind of life. Her stepmom was kind to Victoria and tried to love her. But Victoria couldn't allow the love of her father and his family into her life. With lots of tears and journaling, she tumbled to the fact that she was afraid to let her dad and his family nurture her because she would feel disloyal to her mother.

Her mother was bitter about the divorce—constantly putting Victoria's father down—even though *she* had been the one who'd had an affair.

Deep down inside, Victoria wanted nurturing from her mother, but her mother's love was unavailable. Victoria tried to please her mother, but her mother always criticized Victoria's actions, and they fought often. Without realizing it, Victoria had built up a lot of anger toward her mother.

Because Victoria rejected the love from her dad and his family, she was left with no one but her boyfriend.

As Victoria looked at the love her family had to offer, she began to accept affection from her mother as her mom could give it. For instance, her mother would never listen to Victoria's feelings or view of life. But she could take Victoria shopping, and they could laugh over a funny movie. Victoria began to let go of her anger toward her mother. When her mom said negative things about her dad, Victoria changed the subject, and her mother eventually got the idea.

Victoria began to spend more time with her dad and his family. She loved to play with her younger half sisters, and she could talk to her dad and stepmom about anything because they really listened.

She came to understand those around her and accept the nurturing they were capable of giving. Rather than rejecting the love that was available and looking for love in places that were inaccessible, she welcomed the support and warmth that was now attainable.

Study your own life. Is love available to you? Can you allow the caring that is around you to be enough?

Seek Medical Help

At times, depression can be so strong, it's overwhelming. You can become so depressed that you feel stuck, unable to perform daily life skills. If the negativity surrounding you is so great you can't get out of bed in the morning or you don't want to see or talk to other people, see a doctor. Go to your physician first and get a referral to a psychiatrist. Your depression may be significant enough that you need medication and therapy to change your life. Making and keeping the appointment can be a huge mountain to climb.

Climb the mountain. You are worth it! Accept the positive energy that surrounds you and look for others in the world who are waiting for your love. Receive and give.

Develop Positive Mental Skills

Affirmations will be helpful to you when you are feeling down:

- I am worthy of love.
- Those around me are supportive.
- I will allow love into my life today.
- I will give a small act of service to someone today.
- I am solution focused.
- There is an answer to my problem.
- I have peace in my life.

Journal to find your thinking process. The following list can help you get started

- Are you solution focused?
- Can you find good in yourself?
- Are you critical of others?
- Are you happy?
- What brings you happiness?

Thinking patterns are habitual. Therefore, it takes time to change a pattern. When your thoughts slip into an adverse place, say "STOP" in your head and visualize a stop sign. This halts your brain with two senses: hearing and seeing.

If most of your thinking patterns are negative, you will have a void in your head if you try to stop all of them at once. Replace them with positive distracters like exercising, good music, and listening to motivational speakers. Gratitude and prayer journals are also helpful.

Give yourself time to change. (See Part 4: Practicing the Process. It's the last section of the book and it will help you develop a program that works for you.)

> *"Mental sunshine will cause the flowers of peace, happiness and prosperity to grow upon the face of the earth."*
>
> Unknown

Visualization is also helpful. The more senses you use when developing a mental picture, the more you help yourself. Create a safe place.

Here are some visualizations that work for me.

I hike in the mountains and feel the cool breeze fragrant with pine scent. I hear the rat-a-tat-tat of a woodpecker and the chirp of the robins. The sunlight flickers down through the tall stately pines. I look up and see the trees waving gently in the breeze. They are listening to my innermost thoughts and nodding their agreement. I am at peace as I crunch through the cushion of pine needles under my feet.

This visualization has the senses of touch (breeze), smell (pine), sound (birds), and sight (sun, trees). Make up your own and add more senses.

It's important to tailor the visualizations to your own specifications. Create a safe place. Surround yourself with amenities that are nurturing and promote peace and light.

I love a lush English garden where a brook babbles off to the side. Rabbits, doves, sparrows, and other gentle creatures live close by. There is a modest home nearby, furnished with soft white cushions on lovely wooden furniture. Soft music surrounds me.

You get the idea. Create your own!

Practice going to your safe place daily, when you are calm and rested, so that you will be able to use it to soothe yourself when you need grounding and self-nurturing.

If I am feeling negative, another thing that works for me is to sit in the sun. We have a deck on the back of our house with a south exposure. I love to lounge there and read or talk with a friend. I can feel the light and heat of the sun infusing my being with its radiance. If it's too cold in the winter or too hot in the summer to be outside, sit by a window facing the sun and soak in the light.

Depression can be lessened and alleviated by changing thinking patterns. Can you love yourself? Use your thought stopping and thought substitution to put positivity in your life. Allow yourself to be solution focused. Use all the skills in Part 4: Practicing the Process to help. Find a program that will be best for you. If necessary, seek therapy, or get self-help books on depression. There are some excellent books that have been around for many years that have good, sound healing processes. Be responsible enough to change. Dare to alter your life.

Out of a dead-looking chrysalis will one day come the beautiful butterfly. Its grandeur will come from the trials it has experienced and will yet experience. Its beauty will not be won easily, and it will be cherished because of the price that will be paid.

Trials have refined your being. Struggles polish you as an individual. You breathe in the air of positive energy, grateful for the path you have walked and the internal strength it has afforded you. Look to the end result of your metamorphosis. Your vision will give you courage to continue.

Personal Well-Being Is the Core of Prosperity

Overview Steps:
- Journal your thinking patterns
- Use thought stopping:
  - Say "Stop" in your head
  - Visualize a stop sign
- Find substitute thinking patterns
- Engage in positive laughter
- Give service
- Play
- Exercise
- Enjoy music
- Listen to motivational speakers
- Keep a gratitude journal
- Keep a prayer journal for others
- Keep a prayer journal for self
- Use visualizations:
  - Go to a safe place
  - Surround yourself with peace and light

Part 3

Communication Proficiency

I love meeting people and listening to their perceptions on life. As they relate their life stories, their outlook becomes clear. Each person's view of him or herself and the world is as varied as the stars in the night sky.

Understanding the assumptions of those around us can lead to clear communication with others. It's hard to lay one's own attitudes aside and listen with earnest intent to someone else's slant on life without imposing our own perspective. But understanding a friend or loved one's unique insight opens the possibility of seeing into their soul. What a sacred invitation—to appreciate another's reality.

Approach with caution. Handle with care. Listen with humility. You are standing on holy ground.

Chapter 15

Letting Go of Negativity in Relationships

I do not want to be negative with others.

When I was in high school I had a classmate who never said anything negative about anyone. A few kids called her a Pollyanna. Others thought she was a fake because she was too nice. I liked her, because she seemed genuine and safe to talk to. I knew that what I said to her would be taken in a positive way. I didn't have to be concerned that the things I told her would come back to bite me as gossip from someone else later. I also learned to watch what I said around her because since she never said anything negative, I didn't feel comfortable doing so either.

Creating Triangles

Teens and young adults like to gossip about their friends because it brings a false sense of closeness. If you know a secret about Joe, and you tell it to Sally, then you and Sally feel a bond. It isn't a true friendship bond because you haven't told Sally anything about you, and she hasn't shared anything about herself, but the false sense of closeness is there because you triangulate someone else into your relationship. That's what gossip is all about. As we grow into adulthood, hopefully we let this pattern go because we have learned healthier ways to communicate.

> "My friends are my estate."
>
> Emily Dickinson

After Pollyanna and I became friends, I tried to say only positive things about others, but it was hard. I could do it for a little while, but then I would find myself being critical again. I struggled at first to control this criticism and negativity, but over the next few years, I conquered much of my negative thinking.

There are still times when I slip and am not positive, but those are usually times when I have negative energy inside myself. It has everything to do with me and nothing to do with the person I'm talking to. Don't you find that's usually true for you? When you're being pessimistic, it's probably because of the cynical energy flowing through you.

Releasing Negative Energy in Friendships

Candy came in for counseling; she had just left her boyfriend because he'd had an affair. They had met in a bar and had an instant connection—like in the movies. This wasn't how the story was supposed to end. She felt angry, abandoned, and betrayed—duped because she loved someone who didn't return her feelings.

As an assignment, she began to keep a pocket journal of her negative thoughts and feelings. She was surprised at the amount of distrust and pessimism she found in her thinking.

Because Candy could see her negative thinking patterns, she was able to let go of the cynicism that overwhelmed her life. She substituted optimistic energy that included

- Positive self-talk
- Fine music
- Affirmative visualizations
- Good reading

Candy visualized herself with a partner who would be faithful to her. She deserved someone who cared about her and would be true to her. As she began to date again, she looked for men she was certain would be faithful.

How did she know they would be true to her? You can't ever predict someone's behavior one hundred percent, but you can be reasonably sure they will do the same things they have done in the past. Look at the pattern of their past relationships and you'll have some idea of how they will do things in the future. However, if someone can look at their past association paradigms and is committed to change, their behaviors might be different.

She learned to be cautious of instant connections. Friendships usually develop more slowly, over time. She chose her companions from groups of people who were more likely to be committed to their partners: men who attended her church, her helping hands volunteers, and friends from her cycling and hiking groups.

It took time, but in the end, Candy was successful and found a good friend and life-partner.

Releasing Negative Energy in Marriage

When Georgia found out that her husband was a gambler, she was livid. Her negative thoughts took two divergent paths: she hated men and their lack of self-control, and she was very angry with herself, feeling that she was a fool and had been blind to what was happening right under her nose.

Georgia's anger fueled her to action. First, she worked out the boundaries that would be best for her. She opened a bank account in her name only before she gave her husband an ultimatum: work out a program to quit gambling, or leave. He chose to quit gambling and save the relationship.

Georgia's husband found a therapist, attended a twelve-step program, and didn't return to the gambling.

To erase the negativity inside her, Georgia began to focus on creating positive energy. She infused herself with light by sitting in the sunshine daily and reading her religious and positive-thinking books. She allowed love into her life by spending time with family and friends who cared for her.

As the pessimistic thoughts surfaced in her head, she said "STOP" and visualized a stop sign in her head. That interrupted her thinking pattern.

Then she wrote affirmations like
- I deserve a happy relationship.
- My money is safe and that brings me security.
- Loved ones are supportive of me.

Georgia also developed several visualizations. She pictured herself as insightful and knowledgeable about people. She could see herself understanding and being able to size people up. She began to envision herself with a loving partner without an addiction.

When Georgia could tell her husband was trying to change, she agreed to couples' therapy. They both became more open in their communication. She shared her fears and her husband listened and reflected what she said. He talked about his insecurities and listed the steps he would take to keep from gambling. They planned things they could do together, like country line dancing and cycling.

Georgia learned to
- Listen to her feelings when something upset her
- Talk with her husband about the problem
- Brainstorm solutions
- Find a resolution
- Listen to her feelings again to make sure the solution worked for her
- And, lastly, work with her husband to solve the difficulty

A year later the couple left the area so I didn't see them again, but I did receive a card saying they were doing well. Her husband had stayed away from gambling, and their friendship was stronger than when they were first married.

Releasing Negative Energy Stuffed Inside

Denise had had several lower back surgeries. She came to therapy because her back began to hurt again, and the doctor said that her stress and tension may be the cause. She didn't want another surgery, so she had to find out what was causing the stress.

Denise was a sweet, gentle person who always wanted those around her to be happy. She tried to please everyone around her, always deferring to others' opinions and ideas. Her boyfriend didn't listen. He interrupted her when she started to speak and talked over her when they were with friends. The pattern was the same with her family—they talked a lot, so Denise was quiet around them.

When Denise was a child, no one ever listened to her. She let resentment and frustration build up over the years, but she never had the courage to speak out.

As Denise became aware of the way she suppressed her anger, she decided to change—to do things differently.

Denise began to listen to her own feelings and define them. She came to know that she was a person with good ideas, and she started to share what was on her mind.

At first Denise overcorrected. She expected a hassle or a fight in order to get her way, so she was ready for a battle in order to be heard. That stance caused her just as much stress and tension as she'd had before.

She soon came to realize she could accomplish her goals using positive techniques. She didn't have to be angry and negative to get her way—honest, open communication was far more constructive for her and those around her.

> "We should be too big to take offense and too noble to give it."
> *Abraham Lincoln*

Denise began to visualize herself working with kind, competent people. When she found herself in a dilemma, she took a few minutes to imagine people being kind and respectful. She deserved and would receive wonderful feedback.

She began to share with her family. When they talked over her, she stopped them in a kind way and asked them to pay attention. Through counseling, she learned how to share, listen, and reflect—and she taught the communication skills to her family. They began to work together to understand each other. Her family liked Denise better this way because they knew what she was thinking and feeling. She became more real to them.

Denise had a harder time with her boyfriend. He always wanted to be the center of attention and thought his ideas were the best. He didn't really want to hear anyone else. When Denise figured this out and reflected on the relationship, she could see that she had two choices. She could remain with him and continue to be quiet and angry, or she could move on.

The decision was difficult, but Denise decided to let him go. At first her boyfriend called her many times a day, saying that he would change. She took him back once, and he made an effort to listen to her, but only until he thought she would stay. Then communication went back to the old pattern of him talking and her listening. She ended the relationship and began to date someone else who treated her well.

Denise and her doctor designed a program of physical therapy and exercise which Denise followed ritualistically. Her back became stronger. Denise was sure her suppressed feelings had exacerbated her back problems. She no longer needed surgery.

Positive peaceful energy began to seep into every crack and corner of her being. She figured out how to give positive energy and receive it back. She could stand up for herself in a positive way. Her gratitude for the skills she had learned was inspirational to those close to her, including me.

It is time. The elegant butterfly is formed and beautiful. The protective chrysalis has now become her prison. She pushes against the walls, straining and shoving. The shell cracks and her two eyes peer out through the opening, looking all around and seeing the world for the first time. Delight fills her new being.

Because you are now experiencing the good instead of the negative, you can also begin to see the world in a new light, marveling at the positive energy it holds for you. What a gift!

Optimism Is the Blueprint to Contentment

Overview Steps:

- Journal negativity
- Recognize negative patterns
  - Interrupt the thinking
  - Say "STOP"
  - Visualize a STOP sign
  - Create positive imagery
- See the people in visualization giving positive energy
- Accept the positive energy
- Listen to others
- Reflect their feelings
- Ask others to listen and reflect what you say
- Fill yourself with peace and light
- Feel gratitude for the daily opportunity

Chapter 16

Finding Positive Thinking Patterns

I do not want to be stuck in negative thinking.

There are as many patterns of negative thinking as there are people. Each of us has established a belief system from three primary sources:

- The personality we are born with
- The childhood we lived
- The people we come in contact with

Everyone comes with an inherent personality that helps develop our outlook on life. We have a little grandson that is always happy. I find him around the house humming little tunes as he plays. Another child may have anxieties. A baby might relax by twirling his hair or sucking his thumb. Each person is born with his or her own individuality—like a beautiful garden full of a variety of flowers.

Childhood is a time of growth and development. It's a point in life when your outlook is established and then augmented. If you grow up with fear, you become afraid. If you are exposed to rage as a child, you may later either cower to anger or feel rage yourself. If you are loved, you learn to love. You pattern your life and your relationships after the things you are exposed to in your early years.

As you grow and develop, those around you have an influence on your life. The culture you live in, your social status, your school, your friends, and those you work with all have an impact on you. If you live with active people, you learn to be active. If you are around gentle quietness, your life takes on those characteristics. Once I had a cold that turned into laryngitis. All I could do was whisper, and soon everyone around me was whispering back. We react to those we come in close contact with.

As you read the following stories, look for your own patterns of negativity. We all have them. Being critical of ourselves is probably the one we use most frequently. Judgmental thoughts have entered all of our heads at one time or another. Disaster thinking is another common practice for many of us. "What if the boss doesn't like my report? What if it rains the day we've planned the outdoor office picnic? What if the neighbor's dog gets into my flower bed?" Sentences that begin with "what if" are usually disaster-thinking questions.

> "Bondage is . . . subjection to external influences and internal negative thoughts and attitudes."
>
> W. Clement Stone

Negative Self-Talk

Dr. R. Hurlburt, a professor in the Psychology Department at the University of Nevada at Las Vegas, taught several classes in thought stopping. Each member of the class wore a small pocket-sized beeper that went off at random every fifteen or twenty minutes. When the buzzer sounded, the person had to record what he or she was thinking.

One of the benefits of this procedure is that it helps you discover your thinking patterns. Dr. Hurlburt's method may assist you, too. To perform your own thought-stopping experiment, set your watch or phone to go off every so often. Keep a pocket notebook with you or use your phone to record your thoughts.

See if you can find a pattern to your thinking. Here are some examples:
- You may be dwelling on your negative behavior.
- You may think you're not good enough.
- You may look at yourself as the cause of negative events.

Even if the people around you are positive in what they say, you can still interpret their message in a negative way. For instance, I said to a young mother one day, "I'd be happy to care for your children while you have an afternoon of shopping." She turned to me and said, "Don't you think I can take care of my own children? I don't run off and leave them just to go shopping."

My intent was only to be of service when I offered to watch her children, but she thought of it as negative. If someone thinks you are being pessimistic, analyze it for yourself before you believe him or her. It may be that theirs is the negative thinking, not yours.

There are wonderful books that go into great detail about negative thinking patterns. Use them as reference guides if you wish. David Burns's *Feeling Good, The New Mood Therapy* has been around for many years and is a classic.

Natalie called herself fat. She was bulimic, depressed, and couldn't find anything good to say about herself. She wouldn't consider changing her way of thinking—until she learned that she would pass these unhealthy messages on to her children. Then she became motivated.

When I first saw Natalie in therapy, I asked her to have a physical exam to check her condition or discuss the possibility of medication for her depression. At first she refused to go, so I had to tell her I couldn't see her again until she brought a report from the doctor. She made an appointment, and she and her physician talked about her problems. She began a regime that worked for her.

Natalie joined a weight-loss plan that required her to attend a weekly group. She received a healthy eating guide, and more importantly, as she listened to the others talk about their addictions, she could see that she needed to change her thinking. I have seen the Overeaters Anonymous twelve-step program change lives. Check with your physician to find a reputable group that will work for you.

Now Natalie was ready to change her life.

Success in Personal Life

As I have consulted with people over the years, I have found that many thrive in the workforce but are unable to find success in their personal lives. They seem to be able to get outside themselves in a job setting, but in a private setting, they revert to patterns of negativity—possibly from an unstable childhood—feeling depressed and unable to see the good in themselves.

I counseled a stockbroker, Tanny, who ran several small businesses on the side. Tanny was tall, good-looking, and pleasant to be around. Her business dealings reeked of success, but her personal life lacked direction.

She struggled with depression, stemming from a childhood dealing with alcoholic parents, and couldn't find the good in herself because she didn't *feel* good about herself. Tanny was not willing to change her thinking in order to feel better. She didn't find a solution to her depression because she chose not to access positive thoughts.

The negative thinking patterns from her childhood remained embedded in her and reverberated in her head like an old cancerous recording. She was a wonderful, creative person, but she didn't know it.

Find the positive in yourself.

Think, Feel, Act

I explained to Natalie that many people have the mistaken belief that our feelings create our thinking, and these, in turn, lead to our actions. In reality, our thinking generates our feelings, which lead to our actions.

If you change your thinking, your feelings will change and, finally, your actions will be different. Natalie agreed to modify her thinking so that her feelings and actions would change.

She began to make use of some of the positive affirmations that members of her group used. Her statements were all focused on her body, but that was great for a start. She wrote statements she could believe:

- I have nice-looking feet.
- I have good-looking hair.
- My fingers are long and pretty.

As time passed she was able to augment her statements to include

- I am a good mother.
- I am a loving wife.
- I am of worth.

- I am a good friend.
- I can enjoy the blessings I have been given.

Natalie learned to visualize herself as okay. She wrote several gratitude visualizations that she became comfortable using daily:

- Each part of my body functions like it should.
- My skin covers my body.
- My ears can hear.
- My eyes can see the beauty of the earth.
- I am healthy and strong.

Natalie was a kind, gracious, lovable person. She moved to another city, so I haven't seen her for a while, but before she left she knew that I loved her and thought she was wonderful. She could tell that to herself daily. We talked about her being able to say she loved herself and mean it. She has a divine spark, and she makes the world a better place just because she lives in it.

It was a long, arduous journey for Natalie to get out of her negativity, but last time I saw her, she was in process—putting in a lot of effort and hard work.

"Problems are only opportunities in work clothes."
Henry J. Kaiser

Judgmental Thinking

I remember as a young teen going into the home of a neighbor late one afternoon. She had three children under the age of three. One was crying, another was begging for a cookie, and the baby needed to be changed. The house was a mess. I remember thinking, "My house will never look like this."

I thought of those words again when I had three young children and my house wasn't as clean. Critical thoughts like that always come back to haunt me. If I think, "That person is clumsy for spilling the milk," I'm the very next one to spill the milk myself. What goes around comes around. Keep positive thoughts before you so that you will bring good things into your life.

Bea lived alone in an old family home. She was angry with the neighbors because they let their dog come into her yard. Children in the area walked in her garden. The mailman put some of her letters in the box next door purposefully to cause her problems.

She yelled at the children to stay out of her tomatoes and took the neighbor with the barking dog to court, then reported the mailman to his superiors to teach him a lesson. This kind of behavior was a pattern in her life.

Bea earned a negative reputation in her small town. People stayed out of her way when she was at the checkout stand in the grocery store, and the pharmacist made sure to fill her order promptly so he wouldn't get yelled at.

Fanatical health rules governed Bea's life. She wanted to stay young forever. Family hated to visit because she lectured them about water filters, vitamins, and other remedies. Yet Bea thought she was invincible.

As Bea grew older, she developed multiple health concerns. Her knees and hips gave her problems, so she had to use a cane. Her skin turned a slight shade of blue because she had taken too much colloidal silver. People were polite to her, but she had no friends.

Bea lived a lonely life because of her negativity. She died alone with no one to care about her.

"If you would be loved, love and be lovable."

Benjamin Franklin

Competitive Thinking

From an early age we are taught to think competitively. Western culture is one of independence for the individual. Children experience competition from the time they are very small. Young parents keep tabs on whose baby walks first or the number of words their child says by a certain age. Many parents have the mistaken belief that early development means their child will be the smartest or the best. Children vie for the top spot in the spelling bee or the fastest time in completing a math-facts sheet. On the soccer field only one team can win. Bands and orchestras have the best players in the first chairs.

As adults there is competition to get the best jobs, to make the most money, to have the nicest looking car. The list goes on and on.

Camille wanted to find a preschool for her young daughter. She searched for the best one, spending several months visiting and evaluating schools. She located a good school that would fit her daughter's needs, but it had only ten openings for the next year. She told her friends about all the work she had done, and several of them wanted to apply to the school also.

Camille worried that her daughter wouldn't get a spot for the fall if all her friends applied, and she expressed this concern to her husband.

"Just picture all of the children being accepted," he said.

"Oh," she said, taken aback. "I never thought of it that way."

Camille changed her view. She visualized all the children getting accepted, and they were!

If you find yourself wishing for something just for yourself, to the exclusion of others, flip your thinking to say, "Wouldn't it be wonderful if we were all successful."

Try changing your thinking from the competitive "I win, you lose" to "Let's both succeed." Can you feel a positive energy flow as you do this? It creates a positive feedback loop inside. The more you do it the better you feel, and the better you feel, the more you do it.

Experience the positive energy! There is enough for all. Everyone can win.

> "Your beliefs become your thoughts. You thoughts become your words. Your words become your actions. Your actions become your habits. Your habits become your values. Your values become your destiny."
>
> *Gandhi*

Disaster Thinking

> "Is it that they fear the pain of death? Or could it be they fear the joy of life?"
>
> *Toad the Wet Sprocket*

Do you ever find yourself disaster thinking or looking for the worst?

Zoe was wonderful at noticing this pattern in herself. Her daughter was learning to drive, and as she pulled into the garage, Zoe said to her, "Slow down, you're going to hit the front wall and knock the whole house down." Her daughter looked at her as if she were from outer space, then continued to drive into the garage slowly, and stopped a safe distance from the wall. Zoe thought for a moment. "That was a disaster thought," she said, and she and her daughter began to giggle.

Zoe soon made a joke out of it. She would laugh whenever she caught herself thinking disaster thoughts, and this humor helped her let go of her pessimism.

Find Your Pattern

Keep a notebook and journal your feelings. Use your phone or computer if it's easier. Notice your speaking patterns. Listen to yourself in daily conversations. Negative talk causes negative feelings.

Record each incident, including
- Time
- Place
- Behavior
- Feeling

After you have recorded your incidents and feelings, define your thinking further by journaling the pattern you see. Maybe you are a disaster thinker, or maybe you are critical of others. You might keep things to yourself with internal critical self-talk.

Change Your Thinking Pattern

A group of clients worked to free themselves from negativity by helping each other with expressions like
- Let go and let God (Alcoholics Anonymous).
- Don't go down that road.

Thought stopping and thought substitution works one hour at a time, one day at a time. It's helpful to have a buddy, so find someone to share your process with.

"People will always respond positively to joy and enthusiasm."
Unknown

There are many other negative thinking patterns besides the ones in this chapter. There is no right and wrong when it comes to modifying your pessimistic thinking. Find what works for you. List the negative things you want to change and find alternatives. We can overwhelm ourselves by trying to change all at once, so focus on changing one pattern at a time. Quick change is always suspect, but change that comes slowly will last.

Work on each item on your list for six weeks to be sure the habit is broken. Then go to the next one.

Push, press, twist. The butterfly struggles for freedom. Its antennae probe the air, keeping it balanced and secure. These active feelers give the added gifts of smell and hearing. How grateful the butterfly is for these two wobbly protrusions.

You, also, enjoy a sense of balance with your positive thinking patterns. The world has more symmetry and stability. You enjoy a sense of accomplishment, feeling that your life is safer. Gratitude is yours.

Intrinsic Gladness Is the Passport to Triumph

Overview Steps:

- Journal
- Look for negative thinking patterns
- List negativity you want to change
- Use techniques like
  - Thought stopping
  - Thought substitution
  - Positive affirmations
  - Positive visualizations
- Participate in self-help groups
- Use a friend as a place of accountability
- Change slowly so your change will be permanent
- Work for six weeks before moving on to the next pattern

Chapter 17

Listening Blocks, Listening Aids

I do not want to hear only myself.

If you're not listening, you block positive energy from enriching your life. You can't hear others if you don't listen, but just as importantly, you can't hear yourself. The ability to hear another person is one of the greatest gifts we can receive. Unless we find out what people are thinking and how they feel, we can't really know them, and the vehicle for finding that out is listening.

The marquee of a Christian church close to us has a statement on it that says: "There are some questions that cannot be answered by Google." If we listen to our higher power, we may come to find the answers we are seeking.

"Be still, and know that I am God."
Psalms 46:10

Being attentive gives us the privilege of understanding another person and finding answers for ourselves from a higher power. Why do we like stories? Because stories let us hear what goes on inside someone's head. Observation gives us new ideas and helps us learn about ourselves as individuals, our loved ones, and the world. The gift of listening is priceless.

At times our emotionality blocks our ability to listen. Anger, fear, and sadness are probably the most common, but elated joy can also keep us from hearing those around us.

Anger Prevents Listening

Masy and Joe came in for marital therapy. Masy was often angry with Joe. At times, her anger wasn't in response to anything specific; it was just general negativity. Masy didn't listen to Joe—she discounted whatever he had to say. It was very difficult for her to see her pattern of anger. It was like an invisible cloak she wore all the time.

Masy had several older brothers who had been mean and belittling to her as she grew up. She had ample reason to be angry with men.

Masy wanted to choose a positive path as an adult, but letting the negativity go was more difficult than she thought. She wrote down her feelings in her journal and worked to re-parent herself. When she released her pessimism so she could listen to Joe, Masy felt naked. Anger had blocked the positive energy in their relationship for so long, Masy actually felt very uncomfortable without it at first. Little by little, she began to pull free of it. But it was hard—she stumbled over her feelings in many different situations.

One night, Masy and Joe were out with friends, and Joe told everyone about something wonderful Masy had done that day. Even though it was positive, Masy became embarrassed and angry. Why couldn't he tell about himself and not her?

Masy felt her negative emotions rising, so she took a time-out. She went to the restroom to separate herself from the situation and used several positive mantras to calm herself down and create a more upbeat mood.

- Significant people in my life are supportive of me.
- I feel the love of God enveloping me.
- My angel grandmother's arms are around me.
- I can feel positive energy pulsing through my body.
- Joe loves me and wants the best for me.
- I can nurture myself.

After the cooling-off period, Masy rejoined her friends, deciding to talk to Joe later. At home she told him she was embarrassed when he talked about her. She wanted to share her story only when she was ready. Joe listened and reflected her concerns until she was sure he heard her correctly. Then she listened while Joe shared his feelings. He was proud of her and thought she was wonderful. He wanted everyone to see her as he saw her. As soon as he finished his thought, she restated his side of the problem until he was satisfied that he'd been heard.

Joe learned to be respectful of her boundaries and to share things about himself only. He was gentle and kind during this process, careful not to repeat the behaviors of her brothers.

Sometimes Masy used meditations she'd developed to change her thinking. If she was at home, she went for a walk; other times she used her deep-breathing exercises. Listening to soothing music also helped. As she calmed down, she could talk to Joe about the issue at hand.

Masy felt free as she let go of her anger and became better at communicating her feelings.

> "Whoever suppresses his anger . . . God will give him a great reward."
>
> *Muhammad*

Distrust and Fear Inhibits Listening

Fear crippled Lila. She thought her husband wasn't paying enough attention to her and suspected that he was having an affair. He stayed at work longer than necessary, making her fear even stronger. He didn't help enough at home. She was afraid he didn't love her anymore. In her therapy sessions, she discussed the same fears over and over.

Lila's husband wanted to save his marriage and listened as she shared her feelings. He started coming home from work every day by six o'clock, but it wasn't early enough for her. He was responsible for cleaning up the kitchen after dinner and bathing the children before bed. Even though he accomplished those tasks, she still didn't feel like he helped enough at home. After the children were in bed, Lily and her husband sat together to watch a television show or read. Lila continued to complain that he was inattentive to her, but she couldn't define the behaviors she wanted any more clearly than she had already.

When Lila talked about her family of origin, she depicted her father with the same characteristics she had used to describe her husband. Her mother thought her father was never good enough—the same pattern Lila had fallen into with her husband.

Lila's husband was a kind, methodical person who accomplished every task given to him. He came to therapy for several months, but said he couldn't see that it did any good. Lila never ceased complaining.

One day he decided he'd had enough, filed for divorce, and left. Childhood fears crippled Lila. She had projected all the anxiety from her youth on to her husband, and she couldn't seem to walk beyond it. She lost her marriage because of it.

Sadness Blocks Listening

Angelina's husband of thirty years died of cancer, leaving her devastated and inconsolable. Grief overwhelmed her to a point where she had a difficult time accomplishing daily living skills like remembering to take her blood pressure medicine. Even when she put her pills in a daily-reminder container, she didn't know what day it was.

Her brother worried about her. He and his wife took Angelina to dinner one night. During the meal her brother suggested that Angelina get a puppy to console her. The sister-in-law argued that Angelina couldn't take care of herself, let alone a dog.

The next day her brother asked Angelina what she had decided about the puppy, but Angelina didn't even remember talking about a dog. She was so deeply involved in her own grief that she didn't attend to the things going on around her.

Inattention Can Be a Habit

Not listening can become a habit. It can be a pattern that served one well as a child, but sometimes those practices don't work for adults.

Janey's father was very critical, and as a child she learned to tune him out so she didn't take on the negative aura he continually gave off. When Janey became an adult she still didn't listen. If she and her husband tried to discuss something, she was sure he was criticizing her and didn't pay attention to or hear what he really said.

Janey didn't listen in conversations with others, either. She was always busy thinking of what she wanted to say next, or beginning to talk over the other person before they finished speaking.

Janey's habit of not listening took some time to change. She used a buzzword in her head when she found herself thinking of something else during a conversation. She chose the word "ducks" because she and her husband loved watching the ducks on a nearby lake. Her husband could use the word also when he felt he wasn't being heard. They could even use the word when they were out in public and no one would be the wiser, but they would both know what it meant.

Janey let her husband know when she felt criticized. As she came to understand that he wasn't thinking anything negative at all, she began to relax and see herself in a more positive light.

Janey practiced active listening, or reflecting what her husband said. This helped her listen with more depth. When he talked to her, she listened carefully so that she could rephrase his idea. She continued to do this until she repeated it to his satisfaction. Then Janey stated her next idea, and her husband responded by rephrasing what she'd said to her satisfaction.

This technique was awkward at first, slowing their conversation way down, but it was worth it. Janey struggled to put her thoughts and wants into words. It was difficult to listen to her husband, but as she did she came to understand his thoughts and feelings. They felt closer than they had in years. She loved getting to know herself and her husband.

Active listening also helped Janey because it forced her be an adult in conversation, rather than reverting to the young child who tuned her father out.

Listening Aids

"The beginning of wisdom is silence. The second stage is listening."
Unknown

Listening and hearing involves joy and enthusiasm for life and those around us. I have a group of children I'm associated with who listen to life in many different ways. Shelly listens with her heart. She runs to her mom and says, "I'll love you forever." Yolanda listens to the creatures around her. She adores small creations. When she sees an ant crawling along, she takes it on her finger and calls it her "pet ant." She loves ladybugs and worms the same way. Daisy is almost two, and she loves reading books. She can sit in a pile of books and carefully turn the pages, checking out each one—listening to what the books tell her. Jenny has a passion for Irish dancing. Her feet are always tapping. Lisa and Suzie have fun by dressing up and painting their fingernails.

Listening shows others that you have a passion for something or someone. Eleven-year-old Suzie loved cooking. Whenever a food show came on TV, she paid close attention. Even though she had a difficult time with fractions at school, she was able to figure out how to cut a recipe in half or double it because she was interested. Her little sister learned all about cooking because Suzie taught her.

One young woman I know is incredibly in tune with the birds around her. She loves watching them. She joined the Audubon Society at a young age and learned bird names and their songs. Maybe she likes birds so much because her personality is kind and gentle like the birds. Another young woman, Jaden, spends hours walking the hills of the rural area where she lives. Jaden can spot pheasants, geese, deer, elk, and moose with a turn of her head. She has sharpened her vision by attending to the wild.

We can practice our listening and reflecting skills, but until we listen to the passion and love others have, we can never really connect with those around us. People loved Princess Diana because she cared about them. Think of the countless media pictures of her bending down to make eye contact with a child and hug them. Children knew she would listen because she got down on their level so she could be close to them. Her caring changed the world.

> "All beings seek for happiness; so let your compassion extend itself to all."
>
> *Mahavamsa*

Likewise, if you want others to listen to you, you have to be enthused about your subject. Audiences can usually tell how devoted and earnest someone is about their chosen subject, and they will often tune out an unenthusiastic speaker.

Journal your listening pattern to discover emotional loading in your relationships. Is your energy toward the person you're talking with positive or negative? Eliminate any antagonistic tendencies so positive energy can flow between you and the person you're speaking with. When you find the patterns and see them for yourself, change them if you wish—but remember, it takes time to change a habit.

As you learn to do this, you not only receive the gift of other people's messages, but you also allow positive energy into your life. You will hear new ideas that will enhance your life.

The butterfly's feet butt against the walls of the chrysalis, forcing their way to freedom. They nudge themselves into the air, ready to taste the delicious nectar of the flowers. Their task is to bring the promise of nourishment to this winged beauty.

Your newfound listening skills bring the taste of closeness to you in your relationships. Light and love come in abundance because of your new skill. Savor the positive joys they bring.

Innate Vivacity Is Indispensable to Prosperity

Overview Steps:

- Journal times of not listening
- Look for attitude patterns
- Allow a positive energy flow between you and the person you are with
- Identify internal distracters
    - Use buzzwords to stop them
    - Listen
    - Reflect the thought of the other person to their satisfaction
    - Speak your idea
    - Ask the other person to reflect your thought to your satisfaction
    - Repeat the process
- Find your passion for life
- Let those feelings spill into your relationships with others
- Identify with their enthusiasm
- Develop an attitude of love
- Care for those around you
- Allow happiness to become a habit

Chapter 18

Bridling Emotionality

I do not want to be out of control emotionally.

If you are overwhelmed by emotions, your gifts of positive energy are blocked. You are unable to receive the blessings because you're engulfed with feelings. When you allow this kind of behavior into your life, you become focused on shielding yourself from the outside world with an emotional barrier that doesn't allow input.

Emotionality puts those around you at a distance. They cannot get close to you because you are too angry, too depressed, too afraid, crying too much, or too closed off. You may be so busy being emotional that you really don't get to know yourself—how you think, what you feel, and the way you really want to behave.

People of all ages can have excessive emotionality. Whatever the age, there is usually a reason for the behavior, and it's important to discover what it is so the pattern can be changed.

Emotionality in Children

Torinda, age eight, could cry and carry on at the drop of a hat. If she had a lot of homework to do, she sobbed, saying that no one had as much to do as she did. She would go on to say that the other kids got to play before they did their work. She complained that she could never have friends over, even when she had had a playdate just the day before.

Torinda's mother had grown up with very strict parents, and she didn't want to raise her child that way, so when Torinda cried, her mother would give her some time to play or let her call a friend to do something.

What was Torinda's payoff for her emotionality? She was able to have things her way and get out of her responsibilities.

In counseling, Torinda said she didn't like getting all upset. It made her feel "bad inside." I asked Torinda why she got distressed. She answered, as most children do, "I don't know."

When a child answers this way, you can help them define what's going on by guessing, then watching for the recognition sign, which is usually a smile. I said to Torinda, "I wonder if you get upset so you don't have to do your work." She looked at me and smiled, but didn't say anything. She had given me her answer.

Torinda and her parents were able to talk through the problem to decide how they would handle her emotionality. When Torinda got upset, she and her parents agreed that Torinda would take a fifteen-minute time-out to do some deep breathing, listen to soothing music, and think of something else rather than feel sorry for herself.

I explained to Torinda that our thinking creates our feelings, and our feelings lead us to actions. If she really wanted to change her actions, she had to begin to think differently.

Think, Feel, Act

During her time-out Torinda said these words to herself several times before she did her positive thinking. She wrote several happy scenes that she could go over in her mind until she was calm.

- Going swimming with friends
- Enjoying a day at Disneyland
- Riding a horse on her grandparents' farm

Lack of structure in her daily routine had fostered Torinda's emotionality because she could manipulate her mother. She and her parents set specific times that she would get her work done, and also established free time and dates with friends. Torinda put the information into a chart.

There were a few bumps in the road as Torinda learned to control her emotions, but her parents stuck to the chart, which made Torinda angry at first because she had to be responsible. She felt better as time went on and getting her work done gave her more free time to play.

Self-esteem grows as a child knows they are loved and as they learn to be responsible.

> "Few things help an individual more than to place responsibility upon him, and to let him know that you trust him."
>
> Booker T. Washington

Teens and Emotionality

Parent-teen relationships are another area that can foster emotionality. As a parent, it is difficult to stay cool and collected at times. For instance, Dourine wanted to take the car to go shopping with her friends. Jodi, her mother, didn't like her going shopping very often because she knew Dourine would spend too much money. One afternoon when Jodi was on the phone, Dourine slipped out and took the car without telling her mother that she was taking it, or where she was going.

When Jodi finished her telephone call, she went out to get in the car to pick up her husband Rick from work, since his car was in the shop getting new brakes. Jodi's anger boiled over when she found her car gone. Now neither she nor her husband had any transportation. They were livid.

Fortunately for Dourine, she didn't have her phone with her, so her parents couldn't call to yell at her right away. Rick found a ride home with a friend, who laughed and told Rick about a similar incident that had happened with his daughter a few years before. Jodi was so upset all she could think to do was watch Dr. Phil and order Chinese takeout.

Rick and Jodi were involved in a parenting class at their church. After Jodi watched Dr. Phil, she decided to call their class leader to ask his advice about the situation with Dourine.

The class leader told Jodi that Dourine needed to be accountable for her behavior. If Jodi and Rick were disappointed in her actions, Dourine would feel remorse and guilt, which would help her internalize the need to be answerable for her actions. If Jodi and Rick set consequences rationally, Dourine would be held responsible for what she did.

If, however, Jodi and Rick were over-emotional with anger or tears, Dourine would probably see them as out-of-control. She might feel victimized and shamed, or she could be angry and resentful and shut down.

In any case, she would not internalize the need to ask for the car, and she wouldn't be accountable for her feelings and actions.

Dourine's actions showed she knew she could get away with whatever she wanted. That, in fact, was the payoff for her behavior.

Jodi and Rick talked about how they would handle the situation before Dourine came home. They would remain calm and rational, allowing Dourine to set her own consequence.

Jodi and Rick stood together by the front door as Dourine entered. She was ready for a fight and began to defend herself before Jodi and Rick even said anything. They stood together physically when she entered the room, as a signal to Dourine that they were united, and she couldn't play one parent against the other.

Both parents told her they were disappointed in her actions and said, in response to Dourine's arguments, "What will help you remember to be responsible next time?"

When she could see that she wasn't going to get a rise out of her parents, Dourine calmed down. Her parents kept prodding her to set her own consequences with the question, "What will help you remember to be responsible next time?" She finally pronounced herself grounded from the car for two weeks. (Which was longer than her parents would have given her, but they went with it.)

Dourine was also able to negotiate some "shopping time" with her friends after her grounding, so she didn't have to sneak around. The three of them sat down and helped Dourine budget her money so she would have a little to spend each month. Her mother realized Dourine was growing up and needed to be trusted.

This was a good experience for Dourine. She now knew she could negotiate with her parents rather than just taking matters into her own hands.

If you are stuck in an over-emotional relationship with your teen, it's a difficult pattern to change. A teen is old enough to be included in the changing process. Listening, talking, and working together are vital to the family transformation.

> *"If you want children to keep their feet on the ground, put some responsibility on their shoulders."*
>
> *Abigail Van Buren*

Emotionality in Marriage

When Tom and Susan came into counseling, Susan was continually angry. Her husband, Tom, loved her and wanted to "fix" her problem when she was angry. He wanted to make her happy by doing whatever she wanted him to do, so when she got angry, he always hurried to do her bidding. At times he was resentful—he never got to help just because he wanted to; it was always because she was angry and demanding. Her payoff for the anger was always getting her way.

As we talked about their behavior pattern, Susan decided she didn't want Tom do things for her because he felt obligated to—she wanted him to do things for her out of love. She didn't always need to have her own way. She wanted some give and take in the relationship—mutual respect. She could see that love is best nurtured when it's reciprocal.

Tom began to let go of his reactivity. His part in the change was to help because he wanted to, not because he had to.

Susan wrote her anger down in a journal and could see a pattern. When she wanted something done, she didn't just ask. She got angry. Her mother had exhibited this same model when Susan was a child. If the work wasn't done, her mother berated and belittled her. There had been no give and take in the relationship with her mother, so Susan didn't know how to create any in her marriage. As she began to talk, Susan began to change.

If we can see things and talk about them, we can think and react differently. Susan was able to set goals as an adult and change her childhood view of life. It was better to *ask* someone to do something. It didn't have to be an angry demand.

> "He is not strong and powerful who throweth people down; but he is strong who witholdeth himself from anger."
>
> *Muhammad*

To release emotionality, take a step back, do some deep breathing, and change your thinking. When taking a time-out, give yourself a set number of minutes to be gone. Tell your partner you'll be back in half an hour or forty-five minutes. Then your partner will know what to expect and when you'll be back. That gives you a cooling-off period. During your time-out, take a walk or do some other physical exercise if possible. Breathe deeply while you walk. Breathing cleanses the body and releases emotions.

Change your thinking pattern. Serve others. Look for the good things in your situation. Even the most obstreperous circumstance has some gifts to give you. Find them before you return from your time-out. If you feel stuck, ask a friend to help.

Anger and fear may be guiding you to get out of an unsafe circumstance. Are you in a situation where you are being battered or abused? Check out your position carefully. Ask a trusted friend. Please keep yourself and other family members, like children or the elderly, protected. If you're unsure what to do, seek outside help.

Redefining family patterns can be exhilarating. But at times you may feel resistance because the communication system wants to remain in the old familiar ways. It just takes persistence and perseverance for change to occur. Then peace, happiness, and gratitude for life will attract unimaginable blessing.

Emotionality as Protection

At times we try to protect the people around us from their own feelings. I counseled a family where a young father had recently died of cancer. The mother, Johanna, was grief-stricken—crippled emotionally by his death. She was unable to get out of bed and spent much of her day crying. The children were so busy making sure their mother was all right that they didn't have a chance to grieve the loss of their father. They were afraid they would lose her also.

This doesn't mean we shouldn't have feelings. We need to have our feelings and then pull up out of them. At first, Johanna needed to grieve the loss of her husband by feeling sad and crying, or whatever felt best for her. Then it was important to set her grief aside to return to her children and to everyday life. It's healthy to be angry or cry, but she needed to be able to get back to a thinking place. If Johanna was to fill herself with positive energy, she needed to release her emotions so the light could heal them.

Thinking governs our emotions, and our emotions influence our behavior. Johanna let her emotions determine her thinking and actions.

I think . . . I feel . . . I behave.

Through the help of family and friends, Johanna began to care for her children. Her mother encouraged her to talk about her feelings with her family, and they were able to grieve together.

With the help of their grandmother, the children made a scrapbook of their favorite memories of their father. In the spring they planted the garden just like they did with their father every year. They wrote letters to him and kept them in a special angel box made just for him. The youngest girl, age six, would sit on the bed with her mother and together they talked with her angel-father. They discussed life and asked his opinion on things and decided what his answer would be. He was still part of their lives; they just communicated differently with him.

Feelings are not logical; they don't make sense. They are a state of being, and we all need to have times of feeling. It's only when we stay stuck in our feelings and can't get out of them that we infringe on others and can't receive positive energy.

Take time for feelings. If emotional debilitation is a problem for you, be willing to seek counseling so you can change your perceptions—set a program for yourself to

- Take a time-out.
- Accomplish some physical activity.
- Use deep-breathing exercises.
- Change your thinking.
- Develop a gratitude journal.
- Use visualization to infuse yourself with positive energy.

The butterfly crowds and jostles her way toward freedom. Her long hollow tongue uncoils itself from under her head and pokes out of the chrysalis into the air, bringing nourishment to this delicate creature.

Your tongue also aids you in finding nourishment through love and closeness to others. This blessing in your life will attract those around you with its positive words and enlightened thought.

Inward Serenity Promotes Growth

Overview Steps:

- Find your problem behavior pattern and journal about it
- Take a time-out if necessary
- Do some physical exercise
- Use deep breathing to relax
- Allow gratitude to heal
- Look for some good in a difficult situation
    - Find the gift it holds for you
    - Embrace the gift into your life
- Seek therapy or outside help if you are unsafe
- Change your communication pattern
- Resist the urge to "change back" to old family patterns
- Have your feelings, but work to come back to a thinking place
- Remember that too much emotionality
    - Keeps others from being responsible for their feelings
    - Protects others from being responsible

Chapter 19

Thinking before Speaking

I don't want to say things I may regret later.

We all know people who talk without thinking. This can take several forms. Some people use continuous communication to distance themselves from others, seeming to be in a hypnotic trance as they speak—droning on and on. Others feel a sense of pride as they speak their mind, not worrying about offending those around them. Still others just spout off, letting their emotions dictate their message to the world around them.

> "Never interrupt someone who is doing what you said couldn't be done."
>
> Amelia Earhart

Continuous Communication

I had a professor in college who could say more about nothing than anyone I have ever encountered. His monotone voice made it difficult to concentrate on his lecture.

Similarly, I presently have an acquaintance who goes on and on, talking about nothing until she finally stops herself. As I watch her, I think she knows she's talking too much. My husband says she can say more about nothing than anyone he knows. These people keep emotional distance in their lives by their communication pattern of just rattling on. It's a form of hiding themselves.

A sweet young girl named Cacia, age six, came into therapy because both her parents had abandoned her. Her mother was a drug addict, and her father was a long-distance trucker who couldn't take Cacia with him. Cacia's grandparents were raising her. In therapy Cacia talked and talked and talked. As we got to know each other, she told me she used to talk to keep her mother from leaving to do drugs with her friends. She admitted that, in the end, her mother left anyway. Talking was a way of keeping her close and it had become a habit.

Cacia knew she talked too much because the kids made fun of her at school. She wanted to quit. So we practiced. She would say three sentences and stop to listen to the other person. After they talked, she could say three more sentences. She worked hard to change her habit, and she was successful.

"Listen to people twice as much as you speak."

Proverb

Speaking Your Mind

Others are apt to speak their mind. They say whatever comes into their heads no matter how it may offend someone else. Usually their statements have a negative edge to them. Sometimes they're judgmental and critical of others. They justify their prejudices in terms of being honest.

A lady, Pat, who lived across the street from a friend of mine, would take a few minutes when they were working in their yards to tell my friend about the neighbors. Pat was always up on the latest news and could put a downbeat spin on almost anything. She made sure to tell my friend that Mrs. Jones did not keep her yard up, and Mr. Smith, who lived next door to Mrs. Jones, hated her weeds coming through the fence.

These people also keep emotional distance by their communication pattern. It is not safe to share things with them because they say negative things about others, so you know they'll say negative things about you as well. I am wary of sharing intimate details of my life with this kind of communicator because I know that whatever I say will be given a pessimistic spin and spread around.

Juliana complained about the neighbors in her residence complex. The man that lived in the apartment below her was a drunk, and she berated him quite often under the guise of "being honest." He lashed back by telling her to keep her dog out of his private entryway and placing an old car motor by her stairs. She reported him to the management, saying he put it there just to irritate her.

Juliana got the maintenance man to put the motor in the garbage and then yelled at her neighbor, telling him he was disrespectful. The next day, Juliana found mud smeared on the steps to her apartment. She was certain her neighbor had done it.

After several weeks of therapy, Juliana decided she didn't want to put positive energy into her life. She liked her negativity. She wasn't interested in changing her thinking or speaking patterns. She was proud of her "honesty" toward others and didn't want to let it go.

I felt a sadness as I bid farewell to Juliana—I was sorry to see her continue in her negative vein. Life has so much goodness to offer all of us if we free ourselves to embrace it. Several years later I found her name in the obituaries. She died of a brain tumor. I have always wondered what would have happened to her if she had allowed positive energy into her life.

Maya worked in the cubicle next to Kathy, who was a talker and could think of more negative scenarios than Maya had ever dreamed of. She listened to Kathy at first, just to be polite, but then Kathy continued to talk and talk. She tried walking away, but Kathy followed her. Maya discussed it with her boss who suggested that she tell Kathy how she felt.

Telling Kathy that she didn't like the negativity was definitely out of Maya's comfort zone, but she decided she didn't have anything to lose. Even if Kathy was offended, she might just decide never speak to Maya again. Maya kind of liked that idea.

Maya had committed to be positive in her own thinking patterns, so she shared that with Kathy the next day. She told Kathy she'd set a goal to think positively and wondered if Kathy would like to join her in that goal. To Maya's surprise, Kathy agreed, admitting that she didn't like her negative attitude.

"Will you also let me know when I'm talking too much?" asked Kathy. "My mother tells me I talk her into oblivion all the time."

Maya happily obliged, pleased with the outcome of her efforts.

> "Once you replace negative thoughts with positive ones, you'll start having positive results."
>
> Willie Nelson

Speaking through Prejudice

Prejudice is a cancer on the soul of many societies. The negativity breeds darkness in the lives of many. Those of us who have seen the aftermath of World War II will never forget what intolerance and injustice can do.

I counseled Jada, who came out of a Polish death camp at the age of eighteen. She was older when I saw her, and she had made a commitment to herself in her early life to lay down the paranoia and negativity that had been beaten into her during her teen years. Surrounding herself with light and goodness and keeping her relationships positive had been her quest. She had a successful career in the United States as a dancer and choreographer and retired happily to a life of peace and serenity. She had many friends and a wonderful husband. She was charming.

She and her husband came into therapy not to deal with her childhood pain but to grieve the loss of a grandchild.

I told her as she left therapy that she was an inspiration to us all. No one could top her stories of heinous abuse. If she could be successful in maintaining a positive life, anyone could.

Many of us will not experience that kind of prejudice in our lifetime, but negativity can creep into our existence in very subtle ways that we may not even notice.

> "Better to slip with the foot than with the tongue."
>
> Proverb

Negative energy fends off the positive. There is good to be found in all people and in all situations. None of us is either all good or all bad. We should celebrate our differences and enjoy the variety in each of us.

Spouting Off

There are those who are angry and spout off at others. These people say more than those who are just honest. They spew their emotionality onto all those around them. Some of them may regret what they have said later, but at the time there is no stopping them.

A tongue-lashing cannot be taken back. The words have been said, and they continue to hurt long afterward. Even though apologies may be given, the hurtful words sit in the blackness of the soul to be pulled up in times of depression and discouragement. This is a sad way of keeping emotional distance with others.

Alie was an engaging person. She said she loved her husband and children. But when she didn't get her way, she let everyone know her displeasure with an emotional temper tantrum. For example, she was upset at her husband because he hadn't purchased the groceries she needed to make her special chili. The children were sick with the flu, so he told her he had to care for the children instead. She could go to the store herself. She was so angry about it that she took several of his suits out of the closet, cut them to pieces, and stomped on them in a puddle of mud in the backyard.

Alie's husband decided that was the last straw, took the children, and left her. Not only did Alie's temper tantrum create emotional distance in her close friendships, but she lost her family because of it. Even though she was sorry later, her words and actions couldn't be taken back.

"Control your emotion or it will control you."
                                        Bertrand Russell

Barb's husband was verbally abusive when they got married, but she was kind and gentle and knew she could love him enough to make a difference in his life. Several years and three children later, he was still verbally and emotionally abusive to not only her but the children as well.

I saw Barb in counseling one day, just after her husband had battered her. Her eye was black and her cheeks swollen. She knew she needed courage to leave him, but she didn't have it. A friend of hers took her to a shelter with her three small boys, urging Barb to stay there for the sake of her boys.

Barb left the shelter and went back home. Several weeks later she was in the hospital with broken bones, and her husband was in jail. This time, she stayed away.

As the years went by, Barb let go of the negativity that had surrounded her. She maintained a responsible position with a utility company, purchased a house, and raised her boys to be good young men.

Through the help of the community and her church, she healed. She gained courage and wisdom through her suffering. But no human being should ever be treated that way.

If you are in an abusive situation with an emotional or a physical batterer, leave. Find community resources to help you. Get out! You do not deserve to be treated that way. Protect yourself and your children.

"The tongue like a sharp knife . . . kills without drawing blood."
                                                                    Buddha

Your Communication Pattern

Look at your communication pattern to see how it distances you from those you love. Keep a journal. When you notice something specific, jot yourself a note so you'll know how often the behavior or comment appears.

You can then choose to think before you speak. If you have positive thoughts in your head, you won't say anything negative because you're not thinking that way in the first place. You'll find that the benefit of optimistic thinking spills over into positive thoughts about yourself. It can become an uplifting cycle in your life.

The goal toward intimacy is not a smooth uphill road. We all move a few steps forward and then slip back a little, but each time we run into a valley we know we're higher up the mountain than we were before.

The butterfly has a natural ally in its friend the milkweed plant. Because it has nourished itself on this plant, birds leave it alone—a protective gift of nature for the butterfly.

You also have a gift of nature in being able to think before you speak. This is preservation, a refuge from the storms of life, allowing you to retain optimistic energy and light.

Internal Optimism Invites Intimacy

Overview Steps:

- Notice patterns
- Journal incidents
- Think before speaking
- Think positive thoughts about others
- Think positive thoughts about yourself
- Set a long-term goal
- Be aware of long-term progress
- Be patient with yourself concerning your goal

Chapter 20

Control Versus Trust

I do not want to be in control all the time, but I am afraid when I am not in control.

Receiving an extemporaneous gift in the form of a drop-in visit from a friend you haven't seen for a while can bring you joy and great blessings. So can taking a last-minute shopping trip with your son. Impromptu gifts like this can alter your to-do list for the day. You may have to let some things go so that you have time to enjoy the last-minute blessings that come into your life. But at times we block these pleasures because of our need to stay in control and plan out every detail of an event or situation. Alcoholics Anonymous has a saying:

> "Let go of the life you have planned and accept the one that is waiting for you."
>
> *Joseph Campbell*

This is a message about trusting life, and trusting your higher power. Repeat this mantra to yourself often and send your issues of control into the light.

The Serenity prayer also brings peace.

> "God, grant me the serenity to accept the things I cannot change, courage to change the things I can, and wisdom to know the difference."
>
> *Anonymous*

Erik Eriksen, noted Danish-born psychologist, taught that trust versus mistrust is one of the early developmental stages of childhood. A baby that is cuddled, fed, and cared for lovingly grows to trust. A child living in an unsafe or threatening environment learns mistrust. She tries to control as much as she can because her life feels out of control.

Looking for Security through Control

I once had a mother in therapy who came into my office extremely distraught. She left her children in the waiting room for just a few minutes while we talked. When we came out, the oldest girl, Haley (age six), had stacked all the magazines in a pile. When asked about the pile, Haley said, "I can make my mommy happy if I clean up." She had a mistaken belief that she could control her mother's moods when, in fact, her mother's mood had nothing to do with cleaning.

Difficult circumstances can throw children into situations that cause them to feel insecure. At times, children learn to sense others' feelings, needing to be sure everyone is happy all the time.

Wendy, age six, came into counseling because her grandmother was worried about her. Her parents had been killed in an automobile accident, so she had moved in with her widowed grandmother.

Her grandmother reported that before her parents died, Wendy had been a happy, untroubled child. But after their death, she became concerned about caring for others—almost to a fault. She made sure her grandmother always had a soda if she wanted one, and she ran to get her paper when it was delivered, even if she was playing with her favorite dolls. She hurried to take out the dog and to help her fix dinner. Wendy was always watching, always careful to meet her grandmother's needs, and, in doing so, she discounted her own.

Wendy worked out her feelings of grief and loneliness over her parent's death through art in the sand tray and with modeling clay. She told me that she was afraid her grandmother would die too, and then she would have no one.

Her grandmother told her there was a whole family who loved her. She was the special, lucky one who had been chosen to care for her, but aunts and uncles could help also. She didn't have to worry. She could relax and just play.

Before long Wendy began to let go and trust that she would be taken care of. Through the love of an entire family, Wendy came to know she was safe.

> "Where trust is, love can flourish."
>
> Barbara B. Smith

An adult has a difficult time letting go of control if her childhood was unsafe. She may not trust herself or others.

Trinity grew up in an abusive home. When her first child was born, Trinity vowed to make life better for her son, Derrick. The boy would have the most perfect life she could give him. Trinity rocked Derrick to sleep at night and was there for Derrick whenever he needed something. It was a wonderful environment for a baby to grow up in, but as Derrick got older and asserted himself, Trinity became frustrated. She wanted Derrick to play an instrument in the band like she had done. Derrick loved art and signed up to take a ceramics class instead. Trinity had been a long-distance runner as a young woman, and she wanted Derrick to join the cross-country track team. Derrick wanted to play soccer. He like felt his mother wasn't giving him choices.

Through reading and parenting classes, Trinity learned to give him limited freedom with the choices she presented. She began to listen to Derrick so he would feel valued. Trinity came to understand that both art and music are wonderful hobbies and that if Derrick chose art rather than music, it was okay. She also learned that exercise itself is great for all of us; it doesn't matter whether it's cross-country or soccer.

Derrick tried out for the soccer team and made it. Children are great teachers. As Trinity learned to parent Derrick, she re-parented herself. She gave herself choices and pursued her own interests. Derrick taught Trinity about trust and love of self and others.

> "Live that you may learn to love. Love that you may learn to live. No other lesson is required"
>
> Proverb

A Need for Control Leads to Lack of Trust

From the time our children are born they work to emancipate themselves. The more we trust them, the more they trust themselves.

Gabriella came from a broken home. She loved her children and wanted only the finest for them. Her husband had had an affair, so she wanted to teach her kids how to choose first-rate partners that would be loyal to them forever.

Her oldest daughter was a wonderful musician and a good student, hard-working, and beautiful. She had a boyfriend in high school that Gabriella didn't like. She was sure this young man was dating another girl on the side.

Her daughter loved this boy, but Gabriella talked her into letting him go. Both her daughter and the ex-boyfriend were sad. They really cared for each other. The couple got back together after several weeks' separation, but Gabriella talked her daughter into breaking up with him again. Finally the young man moved on to marry someone else.

Gabriella's daughter is now thirty and beginning to date again. She is working to separate herself from her mother and find her own way in life. She doesn't ask her mother's opinion on everything anymore, and especially not on men. She is learning to make her own decisions.

Will she be successful? Probably. She is a successful student, a good musician, and she works hard at each task placed before her. Since she is doing well in other aspects of her life, the pattern will probably continue. She will move beyond this problem and find a partner she can love.

Relationships between parents and children can be tricky sometimes. As parents, we need to allow our children to emancipate themselves. As children, we need to find our way. Even if we make mistakes, it's okay. My parents and grandparents had problems too, and they learned from them—just as we learn from ours.

"*Peace comes from within. Do not seek it without.*"

Buddha

Trusting

Learning to trust can be a lifelong quest. Trusting requires letting go enough to receive blessings. When you feel a need to control situations and people, learn to recognize your behavior. Have a friend coach you if necessary. Say "STOP" and visualize a stop sign in your head. Then write several mantras or use wise quotes from great teachers you trust:

- I cannot make anyone feel what he or she does not choose to feel.
- Let Go and Let God (Alcoholics Anonymous slogan).
- The world is not ordered according to me.
- I cripple someone if I do for them what they can do for themselves.
- I can only choose for myself.
- Things will happen as they are supposed to.

Deep breathing can also help. Create a safe place for yourself and go there to reduce your anxiety. (See the section on Guided Imagery <XX>.) Look for the middle ground in the situations you are involved in. Stay away from black-and-white thinking. One person isn't right or wrong. If we asked a group of people to solve a dilemma, they could each come up with a different plan, and it would be okay.

If you are having trouble allowing others to make decisions, give them limited choices. Decide what boundaries you are comfortable with and then provide them freedom within your parameters. Look at the big picture and allow those around you some choices, like Trinity did with her son Derrick.

I have a dear friend who jokes with me. She'll say, "I'm not in charge," when her granddaughter takes all her shoes out of the closet to play dress-up. If my friend gets ready to go out for the evening, she might find a ring or a scarf stuck in one of the shoes. She just smiles and tells herself she's helping raise a grandchild, not creating a perfect closet full of shoes.

The greatest gift we can give the world is our love. May we cherish the love we have inside us and give it away one small act at a time.

Many butterflies have brush legs used for tasting and smelling. These little brushes are a blessing to our butterfly, allowing her to ensure that food is found. Security comes from relying on this important appendage.

You, likewise, are grateful for the security of letting your higher power guide you through each day. What a blessing to have this gift of trust in another, who is greater than you.

Self-Affirmation Leads to Internal Peace

Overview Steps:

- Keep a journal
- Recognize control patterns
- Use thought stopping
- Write your mantras and say them often
- Do deep-breathing exercises
- Go to your safe place
- Plan details, and allow extemporaneous happenings
- Find gifts in each situation
- Picture yourself trusting others
- Love those around you

Chapter 21

Self-Responsibility

I do not want to be responsible for the feelings of others.

Whenever we do for others what they can do for themselves, we cripple them. If we become too focused on others, we aren't free to give and receive positive energy for ourselves. Caring about others is a healthy way to live. Caring for others blocks the gifts.

I am responsible for myself, but I am always willing to serve and help others.

Developing Autonomy

Children teach us about autonomy. They strive toward independence. Our four-year-old granddaughter often says, "Don't help me. I can do it myself."

Never do something for a child (or an adult) that they can do for themselves.

If I tie a three-year-old's shoe, that's great, but if I'm still tying his shoes when he is eight, then I have broken my rule: I am caring *for* him, rather than *about* him.

I cripple a child by doing for him what he can do for himself.

Danielle was the only child of an older couple. They were thrilled when she was born and took meticulous care of her as she grew. When she went to first grade, she waited for the teacher to take her jacket off for her, and then sat at her empty desk, expecting the teacher to place her paper and pencil in front of her before she began to write. Danielle had to discover how to take care of herself by watching the other children.

The same dynamic is true for adults. A couple in their late seventies has a son, age fifty, living with them. The son has no job, career, or other family contact. He is living a nonproductive life, and may have a difficult time adjusting to work again when his parents are gone.

"You cannot travel the path until you have become the path itself."
Buddha

China had a hard time setting boundaries. An older sister had always talked for her while she was growing up, so in adulthood she was afraid to tell others how she felt.

China's eight-year-old son was taking trumpet lessons, and his teacher demanded that he practice an hour and a half each day. China's son didn't want to practice that much each day, and a battle ensued. China didn't know what to do, but after fretting about the situation, she decided to look for another teacher.

She found a brass ensemble group her son could be part of, which required only thirty minutes of practice each day. Her son committed to do this, and they made the decision to switch. Now China had to tell the present teacher that she no longer required his services—though she wished someone else would take care of it for her.

China didn't want to hurt the teacher's feelings, so she thought maybe her son could do both private lessons and the ensemble. China's husband told her that was crazy. He reminded her that the reason they were changing teachers in the first place was because there was too much practicing. Their son definitely didn't want to practice for two lessons.

China fretted about telling the teacher. She brainstormed what she would say, then she practiced the conversation.

1. Tell the teacher she appreciated what he had done for her son.
2. Thank the teacher.
3. State her position.

Over the telephone, China told the teacher she appreciated him and was grateful for his services, but their son wanted to take another direction in his studies. China felt great after she solved her problem—she was one step farther down the path of self-responsibility.

Trying to control other people's feelings keeps us from the positive energy waiting to bless our lives.

Finding Your Own Happiness

When we focus on others, allowing negative energy to envelop us, we lose sight of the good in the people we are closest to.

Helen came into my office complaining about everything her husband did. When I asked her to try rewording her statements to be "for" herself rather than "against" her husband, the question stopped her dead in her tracks. Helen didn't know how to think about being "for" herself. She didn't know what she wanted.

She had been so used to taking care of and controlling others that she didn't know how to get in touch with her own needs. She had worried, manipulated, and monitored. She had taken over responsibilities that belonged to her husband. But she hadn't thought about herself.

At first it was a conscious struggle for Helen to decide what her needs were. Each time she was in a bad mood, she sat down to write exactly what she wanted. What would make her happy? At first Helen just stared at the paper, not knowing what to write. Then, gradually, she became aware of how she could care for herself.

Helen's husband was very friendly. He loved to talk to other people—and talk a lot. She told him how she felt and explained that she really wanted to see him in a positive way. Her husband was happy to compromise with her. When they were out with friends, she could pat his knee, and he would know he was dominating the conversation. On the other hand, she also began to listen and interject her own thoughts into the discussion. Time with friends became more interesting to her.

She told her husband it bothered her when he left his clothes on the floor. He said he would try to make more of an effort to pick them up, and she got a laundry hamper that she could throw things in if the mess bothered her too much.

The couple set a time that they could be together in the evenings. Her husband told Helen he liked spending time with her much more now that she was focusing on positivity. They rekindled the strong friendship they had before they were married.

Helen said that turning her thinking around was like scaling a high mountain. She took it one step at a time, one day at a time. After a while she didn't need to write her needs and solutions anymore because she could spontaneously come up with them.

Helen evaluated her life and decided to set new goals for herself. She found it very freeing for her to do the things that she wanted to do to develop her own strengths.

"Learn to know thyself."

Muhammad

Caring Versus Caretaking

We are taught by society and by our families to be caretakers. Humanity looks at women as caretakers, and it is true that females, by temperament, are sensitive. But men also can be very caring by nature, and many of them not only take care of their families but also become health care professionals. Almost all of us, unless we are extremely self-centered, nurture the people around us in some way.

Evelyn attempted to commit suicide when her oldest son was killed in an avalanche, and the doctor put her in the psychiatric ward of the local hospital. Her appointed release date came and went, but Evelyn hadn't completed her treatment plan.

When her psychologist came to find her, Evelyn was down the hall helping another patient with an art project. At group time, Evelyn worked with someone else on a journal entry. She was so focused on others that she neglected herself.

An isolation room helped Evelyn realize the seriousness of her situation, and she began to finish her own assignments. She had spent her whole life working in a charitable job, never thinking of herself. She came to know, through her healing, that she needed nurturing just as much as everyone else.

Helping avalanche survivors and their families became a quest for her as she grieved her son's death. She found a healthy blend of addressing her own sadness while also working with others.

The difference between caring and caretaking is detachment.

Detachment can be defined as steering clear of emotional over-involvement. When we care about others, we hope they are happy. But their happiness isn't within our power to grant. Others can grow and change from the difficulties they experience, but they are the ones who have to make that happen. We can't do it for them. We must honor others enough to know that they can meet their needs and fulfill their desires.

I taught parenting classes for several years, and the last lesson included the following story:

You are out in the lake with your family in a boat when a bad storm comes up. The boat capsizes. Everyone is floundering in the water. Who do you save first, yourself or your children?

Most people answered that they would save their children first. But how can you save your child if you are drowning? You will all go down together.

I have learned over the years to strengthen myself first. I like to relate this process to the safety message given by the airlines before departure. If there is a lack of oxygen in the cabin, a parent must first put on her own mask and then put one on her child. I must find my own life support before I can help others.

What does it mean to put on my own oxygen mask or find my own life preserver? The answer is as varied as the number of people we ask. When my children were little, it was taking a few minutes to read when they were napping, or talking with a friend on the phone after they were in bed at night. As they grew older it was working on a project with a dear friend, or enrolling in a master's program at a nearby university. Consider what it might mean for you.

Kathleen and her family experienced a catastrophic event. Their house washed away in a mudslide in Southern California, devastating them entirely. Priceless memories were lost: Kathleen's grandmother's picture, her recipe for her favorite apple cake, and her children's school projects. Everything was lost in the mud.

Kathleen and her family worked to rebuild their lives after their loss with help from the community and their church. Counseling provided a means for them to strengthen themselves during this process.

Their four-year-old daughter seemed devastated by the disaster. She developed lengthy temper tantrums. At first Kathleen put her on time-out, but she wouldn't stay. Kathleen got angry, and so did her daughter. The crisis counselor suggested that Kathleen cuddle and sing to her little girl at times when she was not upset. The child responded almost immediately to the caring and nurturing.

Kathleen realized that she couldn't take away her daughter's anger, but she could help her work through it by loving her. She cared *about* her child rather than *for* her by allowing her to have her own feelings.

After a few weeks of "love time" (as she called it), Kathleen's daughter returned to the happy child she had been before the tragedy. It was as if Kathleen had put on her oxygen mask so she could breathe, and then helped her daughter breathe also.

> "I beg you take courage; the brave soul can mend even disaster."
> Catherine the Great

Allowing Others to Be Responsible

Ruth let a lot of negativity flow through her. She was angry with her husband and his drinking problem. She brought him in to talk to me, hoping counseling would "fix" him. She threatened that he needed to quit drinking, "or else." She couldn't say what "or else" meant. It was an idle threat, and her husband knew it.

Her communication patterns included the following:
- If she was angry, she would say, "You make me so mad."
- If he got angry, she would say, "I'm so sorry I've upset you."
- When he threatened to leave, she would say, "I can't live without you."

Ruth felt responsible for her husband's feelings. It was difficult for her to see that she could have her own feelings, separate from his. However, she began to do things for herself anyway. She went back to school and took an accounting class.

Late one night when her husband hadn't come home, she knew he was drinking. She realized she couldn't control his every movement, and she didn't t know what to do. Ruth talked with a friend who suggested she must like living with an alcoholic because she continued to do so no matter how often he went out drinking. Suddenly the light went on in Ruth's head. She could control only her own behavior, not his. When he came home, she wasn't angry with him like she usually was. She told him she was sorry he chose to drink. She loved him, but she didn't want to live with his problem anymore. If he chose to continue to drink, he could find another place to live.

Now her husband was worried. He could feel the strength in Ruth's statements. She didn't want to live with an alcoholic, and she could get along without him. She wasn't begging and pleading with him like she had done before. Her idle threats were gone, and he knew she really meant it this time. He got involved with Alcoholics Anonymous and began to work a program for himself.

Things changed in their lives. Ruth began to care *about* others, rather than *for* others. Her communication changed.

If she was angry, she no longer said, "You make me so mad." She knew no one could make her feel any way she didn't choose to feel. So instead, she chose to say, "I'm upset right now. I'm going to take a time-out until I feel calm."

If her husband got angry, she didn't say, "I'm so sorry I've upset you." She'd say, "I'm sorry you're upset. I'll let you have a little time to sort out your feelings." She knew now that he was the only one responsible for his feelings.

When he threatened to leave, she didn't say, "I can't live without you." She said, "I love you, and I would like you to stay. I'll be sad when you leave, but I'll be okay." She knew she was an autonomous individual who could take care of herself.

> "Thinking well is wise; planning well, wiser, doing well wisest and best of all."
>
> *Forbes*

The butterfly continues to squeeze and strain and muscle her way out of the prison of her cocoon. Bright colors are beginning to show, letting the world know that this little creature will soon be responsible for bringing loveliness into the earth. What a gift to be blessed with this added enlightenment.

Through newly acquired self-responsibility, you are also bringing your beauty to the world—all your talents and abilities will make life more enjoyable for those around you. The earth is thankful for your ability to share yourself.

Joy and Enthusiasm Bring Success with Others

Overview Steps:

- Look at your close personal relationships
  - Are your boundaries healthy?
  - Can you function in an autonomous way?
- Talk things over with the person you are involved with
- Work together to solve your problems
- Establish clear, positive communication lines
- Stop negative patterns
- Be sensitive to your own feelings
- Make a list of your needs
- Brainstorm ways to fulfill those needs
- Use positive thinking skills
- Take time for yourself

Chapter 22

Positivity in Relationships

I do not want to have negative energy with my partner.

Entering a relationship is like walking on holy ground. To be invited into the space of another person is a sacred experience. To know the soul of another is a true blessing. Cherish it.

> "Ye will not enter Paradise until ye have faith, and ye will not complete your faith until ye love one another."
>
> Muhammad

There are as many ways to bring positive energy into a relationship as there are people in the world. The following are a few I saw in my practice.

Being Open to New Ways

Sometimes we think our ideas are best, and we want to have everything and everyone ordered according to us.

Josie always wanted things her way and pouted if it didn't work out just how she had planned. She thought the whole world should think the way she thought.

As the youngest child in the family, she'd grown up with everyone loving and catering to her. She had everything she ever wanted.

When Josie married Sam, her life changed completely. She adored Sam, and they were very good friends, but she was angry at the beginning of their marriage because she wanted things her way without compromise. She didn't want to work, or do the laundry, or clean up the apartment.

After a severe temper tantrum toward Sam, she sat in the living room crying. Sam knelt beside her and told her he wanted her to be happy. His kind words in contrast to her angry ones caused her to really look at herself. She decided she didn't like herself that way. She talked with her girlfriends and found they were also struggling with adjustments in their marriages. She realized that she needed to talk things over with Sam if she wanted to be happy.

She told Sam that she felt like all the responsibility of the home fell on her. She was just as tired as Sam was after work and didn't want to be left with all the household jobs. The two of them outlined a plan. They organized the housework so each of them had daily chore assignments. That way they could keep their household running smoothly together, and still have fun.

Josie and Sam were successful in their marriage because both were willing to be open to new ways. I admire Josie because she let go of her pampered life and, with a constructive attitude, learned to adjust and share.

Positive energy found its way to Josie and Sam because of their optimistic attitudes.

At the other end of the spectrum are those who grow up with fear in out-of-control living. Connie was abused as a child, and she had to work hard to please her father. She had grown up in such chaos that as an adult she determined to live an orderly life. Having everything in its place gave her a sense of control that hadn't been part of her life as a child. Even though her parents were deceased, she still felt the pain of her early childhood years.

After Connie got married, she cleaned her house daily. Her husband, Mel, came from a close, loving family where everyone pitched in and worked together. He wanted to work with Connie, but she wouldn't let him. He couldn't clean to her standards. She went into a rage if anything was out of place, and had to put things in order immediately. Everything in her life had to be just so, and she wouldn't even let her husband help her.

Connie planned her day down to the smallest detail. She became tired and frazzled as their children were born and she realized how much work they were. She had a particularly difficult time when one of her children got sick or she had to rearrange her life in any way.

Connie had experienced severe abuse and shame in her life, so she reacted to situations in a negative, angry way. However, she was determined to have a different life than the one she had lived as a child.

She and her husband came to therapy weekly at first, and have returned over the years whenever they've needed help solving a problem. She kept a journal. She also wrote angry letters to her father and other abusers in her life to release the negative feelings she had inside. She then shredded the letters, knowing their true value was in the emotional release, not in sending them.

Thought stopping helped Connie when she got upset. She would take a time-out to regroup and decide where her level of comfort was at the moment. Visualization was also helpful for her. She created a safe place and envisioned the possible positive outcomes of difficult situations. She allowed light into her life whenever she felt negative. She pictured herself being flexible. For instance, if her two-year-old was having a temper tantrum, she would take a time-out and see herself handling the situation with calmness. She could then redirect and give appropriate boundaries in a kind and loving way.

Connie was active in her religion and felt nurtured and cared for by her minister and the congregation she belonged to. She said that those people were like her family, and in a way replaced her abusive family of origin. She became closer to her church friends because they treated her more like family than her parents had ever done.

Because of Connie's positive attitude, she was successful in creating a caring, loving home for herself and her children. Through her hard work, she truly made the world a better place for her family than it had been for her in childhood.

Being open to new ways with a positive attitude brings light and energy into our lives. Both Josie and Connie learned that the world is about give and take, and happiness comes from sharing, letting go, and going with the flow.

"Only love can be divided endlessly and still not diminish."
                                                    Anne Morrow Lindbergh

Safety in Relationships

Assessing the safety issues in your relationship will have two aspects:
- Is your partner a safe person?
- Are you a safe person?

Gwen came into therapy saying that she was angry with her husband. She described him as
- Negative
- Judgmental
- Argumentative
- Unable to keep secrets
- Lacking boundaries
- Failing to listen

I commented on the length of the list, and then asked if she had any of those characteristics herself. She flushed and admitted that she did.

Safety in your relationship begins with you. If you are kind and loving with those around you, they will usually be kind and loving in return. Find the good traits that you see in your partner. Tell him daily that you love him and share specifics about his positive qualities.

Relationships are like mirrors. We see ourselves in others. Look at the behaviors you criticize your mate for, and see how many of the same things you have trouble with yourself. A lady once said to me, "I can't stand my husband. He's too critical." She couldn't see that she was being just as critical herself.

Gianna was angry with her husband because he was so critical. She couldn't stand to go home and had moved out temporarily to stay with a friend. During my first counseling session with her, she spent the entire time telling me about her husband's faults and his wrongdoings.

Since Gianna was a very introspective person, she was able to look at her own imperfections as well. When I pointed out that some of the negative things she said about her husband also applied to her, she was stunned. But as she thought about it, she began to see it.

Gianna began to change, becoming kinder and working on her imperfections. As an assignment, I asked her to make a list of the positive qualities her husband possessed—the things that made her fall in love with him. She came to the next session with a long list that helped her remember his good qualities—the reasons she fell in love with him in the first place.

The relationship mirror works in a positive, as well as a negative, way. As Gianna listed the good qualities about her husband, her attitude and interactions became more positive. If communication became negative between them, she was able to stop and start over in a positive vein.

She decided to ask him to come to therapy with her. Over the weeks, both worked to find the good in each other. Before, they had been stuck in a pattern of attacking and blaming each other, with no forward progress. Now, when problems arose they were able to move forward in a solution-focused way.

Safety had infiltrated their relationship because of their positive attitudes.

> *"You yourself, as much as anybody in the entire universe, deserve love and affection."*
>
> *Buddha*

With all this said, there are situations where a person is unsafe in a relationship. When physical abuse, battery, or sexual abuse is involved, seek professional help. Care for yourself and your family. Keep them safe.

Cherish Positivity

If I want to find love and acceptance in my life, I must first find it in myself.

How do you deal with a partner who is a perfectionist and critical of your work?

Hilary was obsessive in her cleaning and housekeeping demands. When her two-year-old twins got their clothes dirty, she immediately changed the children and put the clothes in the washer. When she unloaded the dishwasher, she took extra care to be sure the knives and forks were stacked neatly in the drawer.

Her husband, Jake, tried to help, but whatever he did wasn't good enough. She was always criticizing his work. Jake grew defensive and they fought over silly things like the nightly dishes.

Hilary wanted the relationship to be positive and peaceful, but she didn't know what to do. One night when Hilary began to demean Jake, as usual, he got angry and decided he didn't want to be treated like a child anymore. He didn't want to say things he would regret later, so he told her he'd be back in thirty minutes. He was going for a walk.

Hilary waited for him to come home, and when he did, she told him she was sorry. She didn't want to be this way. She would try to stay calm so they could discuss the problem.

Hilary realized that she was obsessive in her perfection. She promised to lighten up and asked Jake to tell her when he felt like she was treating him like a child.

They both wrote a mantra to help them keep the positive in mind.

Hilary: Today I will relax and go with the flow.

Jake: Today I will be responsible for my feelings and share them in a loving way.

They each gained a feeling of safety in their relationship because they could talk about their problem and work together to change it. This couple was successful because they were willing to alter their communication.

Safety in all relationships is important. Natalie was an up-and-coming CPA, employed by a successful accounting firm. She had scheduled a working luncheon with an important potential client, and she hoped to convince him to bring his business to her accounting firm.

Natalie's boss, William, had a temper and was known, at times, to intimidate his coworkers. He stormed into her office the day of the luncheon and told her he needed her help to plan a surprise party for his wife's birthday. His daughter was supposed to handle all the arrangements, but she had gone off with her boyfriend for the weekend to the family condo in Palm Springs. William was angry.

Natalie told him she had a lunch meeting with a potential client. William told her that her meeting was inconsequential. He knew that her client wouldn't come on board, and she was wasting her time. Natalie needed to help him with the birthday party instead.

In the past, Natalie would have felt criticized and intimidated and given in to her boss. She would have cowered in his presence and done whatever he wished. But Natalie had just finished an assertiveness training class and wanted to practice what she had learned.

Doing the unexpected, she knew, would catch her boss off guard, so she chuckled. "It sounds like you need a favor from me," she said.

William stopped in his tracks with his hand in mid-air to make another point in his argument. He smiled. "I guess that's right," he said.

"I'll be happy to help you, *after* my business luncheon," Natalie said.

William shook her hand and said, "Fine."

Since Natalie was raised with a critical father, she could have taken her customary role as the whipped child—her boss certainly was the critical parent. Instead she decided to be an adult in the situation, and he responded in kind.

Look for your worth and others will also.

Do you care for yourself? Do you know your value? Do you know that you are of great worth? You are a divine human being, created with an intricate, intelligent brain. You live in a beautiful world with much to be grateful for. As you begin to develop positive thinking patterns about yourself, those who are positive will be drawn to you.

Early in our relationship, my husband and I were locked into negative communication patterns. As I began my journey from negative to positive, our relationship was affected. I quit arguing. I quit always feeling like I had to be "right." I quit listening to his negativity. We learned to laugh at our problems and ourselves. Both of us have since become positive in our thinking and speaking patterns. There are still times when one or the other will slip back, but we are a check and balance for each other.

Journal your negative thinking patterns and replace them one by one. Remember that you have to change your thinking before your feelings and behaviors can change.

Think, Feel, Act

Make yourself the best you can, and those around you will either follow or be replaced by someone better.

"I never knew how to worship until I knew how to love."
Henry Ward Beecher

I love the synergism that develops when I work with others. It is a magical thing that happens in therapy or with friends where the sum of the whole is greater than the sum of the individual parts. The men who pulled borax out of Death Valley found synergism worked for their mules. Twenty individual mules, hauling individually-loaded wagons couldn't pull as much borax as twenty mules working together, pulling one long train. Find an example of this in your own life. Is there synergism in any of your relationships?

Large blue butterflies have the blessing of positivity in relationships. The ants take the little caterpillars to their nests and let them eat ant grubs. The caterpillars, in turn, give the ants a sweet drink of honeydew from a gland on their body. The ants protect the chrysalis and watch as the butterflies break out of their shells and fly away. Both butterflies and ants are better from their relationship.

You also cherish the positivity in your relationships. You nurture those around you as they care for you. The blessing of reciprocity brings the potential for synergy—becoming greater than yourself—into your life.

Deep-Seated Satisfaction is Pivotal to Self-Conquest and Love of Others

Overview Steps:

- Assess your level of comfort in accepting new ideas
- Journal your need to control
- Notice your negative thinking patterns
- Journal them
- Replace negative patterns with positivity
- Use thought stopping
- Take time-outs
- Visualize positive outcomes
- Practice giving to others
- Spend some extemporaneous time each day having fun
- Allow synergism to work in your life

Chapter 23

Feeling Free in Relationships

I do not want to feel stuck in a relationship.

At times couples get stuck in an endless cycle of dysfunctional communication—sometimes called a "pursuer/distancer" relationship. Part of the time, one person will chase and the second person will distance themselves. Then they may change places so that the second one will pursue and the first will run away. Unless new information is infused into the situation, it will not change. People stay in relationships like this because

- It feels comfortable.
- They are afraid of change.
- They are afraid to try something new.
- They don't want to feel the loneliness of ending a relationship.
- They don't see what is happening.
- They don't understand what is happening.

Being free in a relationship means staying in the relationship because you choose to stay, not because you feel trapped or are afraid to leave.

A "Stuck" Relationship

A dating couple does not have as much at stake as a married couple. The rules that govern relationships are the same, but dating couples are free to enter and leave relationships because the marriage commitment has not yet been established. Married couples may have children that need to be considered. Every opportunity to save the relationship ought to be explored.

That being said, at times married couples are stuck in relationships because they do not give themselves or their partners a choice about whether to stay or leave. This also keeps the marriage from growing and changing. Whenever you stay because you feel like you "have" to, the partnership is stuck. But if you stay because you want to stay, the marriage can move forward.

Burt and his girlfriend, Cindy, had been dating for three years. She moved into his apartment after being with him for six months. Then they decided to buy a house together because they needed a bigger area for their black Labradors.

Cindy was thirty-eight and taught high school. Her parents put pressure on her to get married—her mom wanted grandchildren. Cindy knew she wasn't getting any younger, and she wanted children too. When she began to date Burt, she knew he had some problems, but she decided that he was the best she could do.

Burt was a complainer, always looking for the negative in situations. Everyone was "out to get him." He was paranoid about leaving home. If they went away for the weekend, he had to hide his guns and his watches. He was sure someone would rob him, but he didn't want to spend the money for an alarm system.

Cindy's dad was as negative as Burt, and Cindy had argued with him all her life. Now she argued with Burt, but he always had the last word. Sometimes she wondered why she stayed with Burt, but she guessed it was because she felt comfortable having someone to fight with—even though she hated doing it.

Cindy pressured Burt about getting married and having children, but Burt wasn't sure. Cindy threatened to leave because he hadn't proposed after three years. She moved in with a girlfriend, but after being gone for twenty-four hours, she called Burt. Cindy had become the pursuer.

The couple had another fight, and Cindy left on vacation with her parents, threatening never to come back. Burt called her every day. He missed her and needed her. Now Burt had become the pursuer. How could she leave him?

Cindy didn't have the courage to leave Burt because she didn't want to be alone.

Burt wanted a pleasant relationship, and, even though they argued, Cindy was better than some of the "crazy" girls he had dated. He decided he had better stick with her. He didn't know if he loved her or not, but this relationship was better than ones he'd had in the past.

A counselor suggested that they each find a therapist to work with before they made any big decision about their relationship. Burt was sure a therapist would talk Cindy into leaving him, so he refused to go and tried to talk Cindy out of going also.

Cindy continued to live with Burt, but she began therapy alone—even though he didn't want her to. Since she felt insecure and didn't know what life held for her, she made a list of the things she could do to work toward becoming the kind of person she really wanted to be, and she started to read positive thinking books.

As a youth she had left her family religion, but now she wanted to get back to it. She found a church in her area and began to attend. She joined a group of single friends involved in service projects and loved working with them.

As the months went by, she allowed herself to receive love and blessings of positive energy. She received an offer to teach at a private school on the east coast, but she had to think about her decision before making it. She listed her short-term and long-term goals. There was a church in the new area with a group of singles.

Cindy didn't know what would happen to her relationship with Burt. She could see two ways that it could develop.

Possibility #1: Burt would feel uncomfortable with Cindy's newfound strength and positive demeanor. It would unnerve and frighten him at first, but his relationship with Cindy would be important enough to him that he would begin his own healing program through therapy, a self-help group, a positive reading program, involvement in a community service group, or a religious group. Both he and Cindy would become stronger people, and their communication would improve so their love could blossom. They would grow and change together.

Possibility #2: Burt would feel uncomfortable with Cindy's newfound strength and positive demeanor. He would become more fearful than ever and fight with Cindy even though she would not fight back. If she moved out, he would think she would call. But she wouldn't. He would call her many times a day and beg her to return. She would tell him if he chose to begin a positive improvement program, she would love to continue the relationship.

Burt walked path number two. He became more suspicious than ever. He tried to fight with Cindy, but she wouldn't fight back. He got depressed.

It was hard for her to see him so down because she loved him so much. She hurt inside because she could see his pain. Her self-help group was very supportive of her, and a dear friend sat with her late one night so she could talk through her feelings.

Burt was angry and met a girl at a bar that listened to him sympathetically. He invited her home—to the home he shared with Cindy.

Cindy was jealous and upset. How could he do this to her? How could he find happiness when she was struggling inside? She discussed this with her therapist and realized he hadn't done anything to her. He was trying to control and manipulate her with his actions. He wasn't going to be any more contented than he had been before.

Cindy was at a higher level of functioning because she understood more about relationships. At first, Cindy had only fleeting moments of happiness and strength, but as time passed both gifts were present in her life more and more often.

Cindy made the choice to accept the job at the private school in the east and leave the relationship. There was a period of grief where sadness seemed to envelop her when she thought about Burt. But in the long term, she did find happiness without him.

This couple couldn't enjoy the blessings of positive energy because of the negative energy surrounding them.

> *"Success and happiness are not destinations, they are exciting, never-ending journeys."*
>
> Zig Ziglar

Gifts of light and positive power can come into relationships in rich abundance. Words alone are not enough to express the abundance that love can bring.

A Relationship with an Addiction

Patty and Adam had been married for twenty-five years. Adam was sure he had a happy relationship with Patty. They spent time together as a couple and enjoyed the strong relationships they had with their children. Patty went back to school when the children were older. She wanted to finish an MBA to give her more options in the workplace. Adam knew Patty needed time to study, so when she told him she was at the library, he believed her. But she spent more and more time away from home. They seemed to have less money than they did before, and Adam couldn't understand what was happening.

Adam followed her one night and found her gambling in a casino. He waited six hours until she came out and confronted her. She got defensive and wouldn't talk.

Adam didn't know what to do. Patty stayed home for several days, but then was gone all night. She came home smelling like smoke, so Adam knew where she'd been.

Adam loved his wife and wanted to make the marriage work, but he didn't know what to do. He felt helpless. He sought counseling to sort out his feelings.

He learned two rules about relationships:

The person whose behavior is the most deviant has the power.

The person who wants the relationship the least has the power.

Adam loved his wife, and he wanted his children to have an intact family, but he felt cheated on because of her gambling. He was afraid to stay and face potential bankruptcy. Adam decided he needed to rebalance the power, so he told Patty that he loved her and wanted to remain married if she would quit gambling and begin to work some kind of program. He didn't care what—Gamblers Anonymous, therapy, anything that would help. She could choose.

Patty said she didn't want to quit gambling and moved out. Adam paced the floor in anger. He wanted her to stay—he and the children were lonely. After a few days Patty called. She was lonely, too. Adam's heart skipped a beat; maybe she would come back. She began to call him every night just to talk. One night after she'd been gone for a month, she said she had spent all her money. She had lost her job and didn't have enough to pay her rent. Adam told her he was sorry, and he would love to have her come back if she began to work a program.

Working a program was not part of Patty's agenda. She hung up angry. Adam was devastated. He wanted her back. Several weeks later, Patty called from a homeless shelter to tell Adam she had been to a GA meeting and wanted to come home.

Adam couldn't understand why she had waited so long. He didn't know if he could trust her, but he took a deep breath and told her she could come. Their small children welcomed her with open arms, but their teenagers were angry. Gradually the family began to repair itself. Adam attended a codependency group to show support of Patty and make sure he was on the right track.

The entire family went to counseling. They learned to talk about their feelings and, if there was a problem, negotiate a compromise. Everyone learned to be responsible for his or her own actions. Everyone owned his or her own feelings and was responsible for his or her behavior.

Healing was a slow and steady process. Every person in the family became wiser and stronger. Gifts and blessings came to them. Adam was grateful for his family. He knew it was the greatest blessing he could have been given.

> *"If you love something set it free; if it returns its yours forever, if not it was never meant to be."*
>
> *Proverb*

Working Together

Many people come to counseling wondering whether to stay in a relationship or leave it. No one can make that decision but the couple themselves. I would never tell someone what they should decide, but here are two principles that may help:

- If two people are willing to work on a relationship, the problems can be solved.
- If only one person is willing to change and grow, the relationship may not last.

Tina and Sean had been dating for five years. Sean's business involved a lot of travel, so he only really had time to see Tina on the weekends when he was in town.

Tina's father had left her mother to have an affair when Tina was young. Tina had always thought—just like her mother—that she didn't deserve someone who would love her and cherish her.

When she took a psychology class in college, she decided she wanted someone who would take time for her.

Tina asked Sean to come to counseling with her. He refused, saying that he was fine and didn't need to be "fixed." That she was the one with the problem. Tina loved positive thinking theories and studied them intently. Tina gained confidence in herself as she studied and told Sean she wanted more time with him. Sean still didn't put forth any effort to be with her, so Tina moved on.

Tina felt betrayed, but she was grateful she gained enough courage inside to free herself. She has since found a wonderful man who is now her husband. They work together and enjoy spending large amounts of time with each other.

There are many other situations where couples have long periods of separation and make do the best they can.

There is no right or wrong way for a couple to arrange their lives and circumstances. Each partnership will have a different way of solving their problems and living their lives. Isn't that wonderful? It's like a beautiful flower garden with an infinite variety of blooms or the variety of beautiful butterflies. How dull it would be if we were all alike.

When only one person is willing to change and improve, the relationship cannot be saved. But if two people are working toward growth and intimacy, most problems can be overcome.

Willa and Henry had been married ten years when Willa found out that Henry had been using Internet pornography. She was distressed and didn't know what to do. Her best friend and her minister both advised her to leave.

When Willa talked with Henry, he was immediately sorry. He told her that he wanted to quit and needed help, then called a counselor and began to work on his problem. Willa came to therapy for herself as well. With the help of a friend, she was able to set up blocks on the computer so Henry's porn sites were no longer available, and she learn how to check the history of the sites visited each day.

Henry worked hard to let go of his problem. He and Willa spent time together talking over their issues and communicating about goals in their lives. They found a church where the clergyman would work with Henry instead of just condemning him. Both of them wanted to pursue their spiritual goals, knowing that God could help their relationship heal.

When asked if she was grateful for her trial, Willa answered that she would have said "no" the year before—when she started counseling—but now things were so much better in their relationship that she had to say "yes." She and Henry had pulled together through their problems and were grateful for the added insight and depth of love that had come to them.

Both Willa and Henry were willing to work on their relationship, so they were able to solve their problems. They were in the relationship because they chose to be, not because they had to be.

Every couple has problems, and no marriage survives without some trials. When two people come together, there is a process of blending their lives that brings up times of discussion and compromise.

> "Those wearing tolerance for a label call other views intolerable."
> *Phyllis McGinley*

Lean, push, tear the chrysalis away! Bright, wet wings wiggle. Blood pulses through them. The butterfly opens them as she basks in the warm summer sun. The wings dry and harden. The tiny egg, turned to caterpillar and now to butterfly, has achieved her final goal: freedom to fly free, bringing pleasure and beauty to all those around her.

You have found your wings, ready to become the person of your dreams, laying down the shackles and prison walls surrounding you. What a gift you are to the world! What a blessing to those around you!

You are Becoming Free.

Internal Peace Summons Joy in Relationships

Overview Steps:

- Identify the problem in your relationship
- Seek outside information by using
    - Therapy
    - Self-help group
    - Religious support group
    - Positive thinking books
    - A program to strengthen yourself
- Read, study, talk, journal
- Give yourself time before making life-changing decisions
- Think before you act
- If children are involved, do everything possible to save the relationship

Part 4

Practicing the Process

I am always looking to find peace and beauty in my life. Sharing that process with others is one of the greatest joys of my life. I find new insights as I talk with people about living. Enjoy the following pages of ideas and wisdom I have collected over the years. I give them to you with my best wishes for positive energy and light to bless your lives.

I once heard a talk at the graduation of an international business school that said if successful people run into a wall, they create a door. If they can't see, they make a window.

What does that mean in your life? Do you have any doors and windows that you need to create? In doing so you open yourself and your life to goodness, so it may give you your desires and dreams.

If you find a wall, create a door. If you can't see, craft a window. Use the techniques that follow in this section to produce doors and windows in your life. Be positive and find solutions. Allow success to come into your life.

Chapter 24

Keys to Success

Think, Feel, Act

Although this technique has been discussed earlier in the book, the concept is important to internalize and act upon if you want to change your life. It is presented again in this section as an approach that is important to healing.

Most of us make the common mistake of believing that our feelings create our thinking. We can allow our feelings to take charge of our lives, but then we have no direction or goals. Our feelings pull us this way and that without any plan as to the path we should follow.

Recent research on the brain indicates that we can change ourselves and our lives with our thinking and experience. Generate the life you want to live—your dream—by modifying your thoughts to create feelings and actions congruous with the existence you desire.

This section of the book is devoted to methods that will show you how to alter your thinking, feeling, and actions—all aspects of your life. Let these techniques become part of you. They are the keys to accessing positive light.

List Your Daily Successes

Keep a journal of your daily accomplishments. Take ten minutes each night to list a few good things about yourself. They might be things you have accomplished. They might be your beautiful eyes or your smile. Your gratitude might be your good thing for the day.

When I counseled children, I would give them an assignment to tell their mom or dad three good things they did each day.

I asked them to think of little things, such as

- I set the table for dinner.
- I fed the dog.
- I drew a pretty picture.
- I read a book.
- I played with my friend.
- I cuddled with my mom.
- I snuggled with my dad.

It was surprising what a difficult task that was for some of them. As adults, the difficulty of that task does not decrease.

Find your own positive list:

- I smiled at someone.
- I hugged my wife.
- I picked a rose.
- I got to work on time.
- I read a good book.

Because you know this will be part of your nighttime routine, look for the positives in your life as you go through your day. Talk about your positives at lunch. Listen to others share their successes.

Positive Speaking Patterns

Create optimistic speaking in your life.

Are you positive and solution focused, or do you always find a "but" when others praise you?

I had a wise client, Marsha, who cared for a foster child, Cassandra. Every time Marsha complimented Cassandra, the little girl said, "Yes, but . . ." and made an excuse as to why she was flawed.

Marsha finally told Cassandra, "Buts to the bedroom." Cassandra had to go to the bedroom until she could say "Yes" or "Thank you" to Marsha.

If you find a "but" for the good you hear, you are disqualifying the positive statement. You cannot be positive or solution focused with "but." It keeps you stuck and unable to move forward. Remember "Buts to the bedroom." Be positive and solution focused.

Chapter 25

Meditation

A friend once said to me, "I can't meditate. My mind jumps from one place to another, and I can't control it."

Meditating is like focusing a camera. Blurry vision becomes clear as you adjust the lens, centering your attention on one thought or one image.

Take a little time for yourself—it could be a few minutes or as long as you would like, depending on your goals and your time frame. Find your favorite place and get comfortable. Maybe you have a big over-stuffed chair that you love to relax in. Do you enjoy being in the sunshine? Is the patio your favorite place? Walking in the woods is a place I love. Relax, get comfortable, and just enjoy being.

Ponder. It's a new journey, a new arena to explore. Focus on a specifically pleasant idea or memory. As your mind strays from your central thought, notice the wayward idea. Is it something you need to address, or can you turn it into a sunbeam of light and send it off to brighten the world around you?

Give yourself time to become familiar with the art of meditation. Study a meditation book of your choice. Let the process be a peaceful passage for you. Let it flow like a serene journey into relaxation.

Definitions for Meditation

So we'll all be on the same page, here are a few definitions and tools that will aid our discussion concerning meditation.

Meditation refers to a great variety of techniques used to promote relaxation, contact a spiritual guide, allow one to get closer to one's own positive thinking, and develop love, patience, forgiveness, and many other mental destinations. Those practiced in the art are able to focus their concentration in an effortless manner for a variety of objectives.

Mantra, for our use here, is a phrase or group of words used to develop a desired mental transformation when repeated over and over. This phrase can be an expression from a religious work or a great teacher, or one you have written yourself.

Guided Imagery is a created message with images, used as an intervention communicated to the mind.

Self-hypnosis is a state resembling sleep, induced by one's own suggestion, where one becomes increasingly unaware of one's surroundings. In this state, one is able to give the psyche believable suggestions.

Breathing helps you bring yourself to a state of relaxation. Breathe through your nose and exhale through your mouth. Breathe down into your belly. Your chest should be still. Count to three as you breathe in through your nose and then count to three as you exhale through your mouth.

Music can aid your process and enhance your visualization.

Scripts for guided imagery and self-hypnosis can be purchased at any bookstore or online. There are hundreds of different types of scripts to help you improve your self-esteem, stop smoking, visualize a healthy body, and so on. Writing your own script is a wonderful method that will help you focus on your goals and retrain your mind.

Creating Your Visualizations

Your mind can't tell the difference between what is real and what is imagined.

You might begin your visualization or meditation in a favorite place in the house. Choose somewhere you won't be disturbed. You could have some soft music playing in the background, and you may want to fill the room with a favorite aroma that relaxes you. Now get comfortable. Lie down or settle into a chair—whatever is best for you.

Begin to focus by playing a meditation tape that you love, or create your own script. (See the following chapter on writing your own script.)

As you begin to put words to your script, say them slowly, pausing as you picture each phrase to allow your mind time to settle on each picture you create. I've included some possible words you can use for a script, but you are free to write your own.

Start your focus by ascending a staircase. Use a soothing voice as you talk to yourself. "I step up onto the first stair, and I feel relaxed. I step up on the second stair and I feel calm. I am aware of my breathing: in and out, in and out." Continue until you have ascended ten stairs.

"At the top of the stairs I see a beautiful meadow full of spring daffodils. They are waving in the breeze. I am filled with the light of the sun shining down on me. I am at peace." Use a visualization that works best for you. Speak the message that you would like your mind to receive.

When you have focused on the mantra you wish your mind to accept, descend the stairs slowly, one at a time, filling yourself with peace and love as you go. Take a few minutes after you have finished to continue your deep breathing and allow yourself to come back to your comfortable place, stress free and serene.

Here are two of my favorite visualizations.

Mountain Trail: I am walking up a trail through a wooded area. I come out into a meadow filled with light and a cool breeze. There is a wild raspberry patch off to the right. It is August, so the berries are ripe. I can taste the juicy sweetness on my tongue and smell the aroma. I pick through the patch, eating until I am satisfied, then continue up the trail. The meadow is thick with tall sunflowers nodding in the breeze. The mountain air is cool and refreshing. There is a gentle breeze blowing through my hair. A small stream gurgles off to the side of the trail, becoming smaller as I hike up the hill. The water is crystal clear, and I can see fish swimming around in it. I continue to hike. The smell of pine surrounds me as I continue up the mountain. Soon I am at the top. I can look down into the valley below. I am on top of the world. I feel peace. I love the beauty of the world. I feel connected with the earth. I am nurtured.

Family Forest: I am walking in the woods above our cabin. I especially love this one because I am walking the trails that I know my father and grandfather walked. Sometimes I go at dusk and small rabbits scurry into their holes as I walk by. I see a deer in the distance. It looks at me and I look back. The forest is dense and the tall pines whisper high above me. They are waving to acknowledge my presence. I know the generations before me have seen these pines. I am close to those who have gone before me. They are with me. We talk. The smell of the forest relaxes me. I am with nature.

Visualize yourself being nurtured by a wise mentor. See yourself in the midst of your dream. Become familiar with the elements surrounding your goal. If you make it part of your inner vision, it will become part of your external vision as well.

Visualizations with Children

I first came to see the power of guided imagery through children. Jessica came into therapy because she was experiencing bad dreams. I had her keep a notebook by her bed so that she could draw her dreams. Each week when she came to therapy she brought the pictures so she could show me how scary they were.

I asked her to sketch a happy ending for each dream. That was hard for her at first, so we brainstormed ideas for positive conclusions together. After Jessica practiced finding a few happy endings, she could create them on her own when she woke up from a bad dream. She loved doing it and turned it into a game. Soon the bad dreams were gone. She healed herself with her positive imagery because she took an active part in her mental process.

Guided imagery also helped children who were failing. A young girl, Tanya, had poor grades in math. I asked her to see herself as successful in class. At first she thought this was a "stupid" idea, but as we got to know each other, she had fun with the visualization. She pictured herself raising her hand because she knew the answer when the teacher asked a question. Tanya imagined herself getting a test back with an A on it. She began to change her thinking, and then her feelings about math changed. Her attitude about studying transformed—what used to be a battle with her parents turned into a positive experience. As her image of herself changed, she changed with it.

Children are excellent at creating their own guided imagery. They love to put their troubles in a bubble and float them away. A worry balloon is able to take their concerns to a guardian angel or an imaginary helper. Strength can come to them from a pretend friend. Sometimes they can make-believe a wizard will shrink their dream monsters into miniature toys, or they can imagine feeding a scary monster a popsicle or a favorite doughnut.

I once talked with a mother who was at her wits end because her six-year-old was afraid of frogs jumping at him from the bushes. She tried to reason with him by telling him there were no frogs in their backyard. She explained that frogs were good because they ate pesky flies. Nothing helped. I suggested she have her son use his imagination to get rid of them—after all, the fear was in his mind. Together they invented green, frog-trapping slime. It caught all the frogs—in fact, it turned into a fun game—and the fear left.

Children's minds are wonderfully creative. We as adults can gain wisdom from their ways.

"No man stands so tall as when he stoops to help a child."
Abraham Lincoln.

Chapter 26

Writing Your Own Script

I've included a chapter on writing your own script because the best healing comes from creating the scene and writing the words that are just right for you. When I worked with clients, I allowed each person to design his or her own visual. For the person to really heal, the words needed to come from within.

Getting the Words Right

Along with outlining your own script, you will want to write some mantras to help your healing process. It's important that you use words that are important to you. Sometimes my clients would ask me to help them come up with the phrases, but I could never get the words just right. They were the only ones who knew their inner feelings, so they were the only ones who could write the healing scripts. The words need to speak to your deepest wounds to mend them.

For example:

Margie's father had been killed in the jungles of Vietnam, and she felt abandoned by her father.

Here are a couple of her mantras:
- My father will be with me forever.
- I have a loving relationship with my father.

As she healed, Margie began to see herself with a significant partner who wouldn't leave her. She had fun writing scripts for this also.

Her mantras included phrases like
- I deserve to be cared for.
- I am lovable.
- I am worthy of a loving relationship.
- I deserve someone I can trust.

I thought she made a great list, but she wasn't finished. She wanted the list to include God, her guardian angel, and her father.
- God will care for me.
- God will keep me with him always.
- My guardian angel loves me.
- I can trust my guardian angel.

I could tell Margie had her words just right because tears came to her eyes as she said each phrase. The words spoke to the depths of her soul.

With guidance, Margie's own inner wisdom held the healing power.

I am always humbled as I work with someone like Margie. It reaffirms what I already know. Healing—true healing—comes from within.

> *"If you wish to know the road up the mountain, ask the man who goes back and forth on it."*
>
> *Zenrin*

A Wandering Mind

Sometimes your mind may wander. That's okay. Let it go where the thought is. Do you need the idea right now? Is it wisdom or just prattle? Accept it as part of you and gently float it back into the world as a bubble of light.

It's difficult to turn off a racing mind. It's like an untamed wild horse, running off in every direction at once. When you find your mind letting go of focus, don't be critical of yourself. Just quietly glide the thoughts out of your mind. Give them to the world as a gift of light. Return to your focus.

> *"A wandering thought is itself the essence of Wisdom—Immanent and Intrinsic."*
>
> *Milarepa*

> *"I was trying to daydream, but my mind kept wandering."*
> — Steve Wright

Reality-Based Visualizations

Lots of people use an enjoyable memory from their childhood. If your family home wasn't pleasant, look elsewhere. What about a favorite aunt or uncle? Was your grandparents' home a place of love? Maybe a friend down the street lived in a caring environment.

My grandfather used to take me to the cattle auction, so I created a visualization with my grandfather, the auctioneer, the bidding, the animals, and a fun lunch afterward. It's one of my favorites.

Maybe you've been on a great vacation, and you'd like to use that. Watch a travel show and create a wonderful holiday meditation. Taking a mental vacation is one of my favorite ways to relax. The sky is the limit. Anywhere, anytime, with anybody is great. Be creative.

> *"It's never too late to have a happy childhood."*
> — Tom Robbins

Visualize creating a peaceful home or room. Decorate it in your favorite colors with a comfortable place to sit and relax. Fill your safe place with things you love, like good music, books, art, and anything else you would like.

Fantasy is popular today. I love the creativity it engenders. Make your own world; envision your own place. Let your mind be free to give you what it will.

Enhance Your Visualizations

Sensory Input

The visualization will take on added meaning and depth if you use as many sensory elements as possible:
- The beauty of the ocean
- The sound of the waves lapping against the shore
- The smell of the salt in the air
- The feel of the breeze blowing through your hair
- The touch of the sand beneath your feet

- The warmth of the sun penetrating into your soul
- The sound of birds overhead

Make it your own, just as you would like it. If you are feeling overwhelmed, make the picture simple and serene. Let yourself be nurtured.

Relaxation

When you find yourself tense and stressed, teach your body a relaxation exercise. You can be creative with this also. Make it up any way you like. I am fond of visualizing myself lying down with clear water washing around me, beginning with the crown of my head and slowly supporting my body down to my toes. The water holds me, relaxes me, and nurtures me.

Here is another technique that I find helpful when I am resting: tense your toes and count slowly to ten, then relax them. Next, tense your feet and relax them, then your ankles, continuing slowly up the body until you reach your head.

Visualize yourself having a massage or lying in a mud bath. Take a mental visit to an expensive day spa with all the amenities.

Create a Wise Mentor

Craft a wise counselor or teacher. I had a client who would ask herself, "What would Christy tell me to do?" She used me as her inner wisdom, and as time went by, she came to know that the insight was really from herself, not from me.

Look for an inner guide in your life. It may be a wise person you have known. Maybe it will be a famous humanitarian like Mother Teresa. Ask yourself, "What would Mother Teresa do?"

What about a guardian angel? Is there someone from heaven, maybe a saint or someone from another life, that could be your tutor? What about a former historical figure? The choice is yours according to your belief system.

> *"If you do not get it from yourself where will you go for it?"*
> *Zenrin*

Create a safe place and have your wise one meet you there. Talk with him or her as if you are meeting for the first time, because you are. Get to know each other. Ask about him or her and answer about yourself. As the two of you become friends, share your problems and ask for advice. Your wise one will guide you.

> "We have what we seek. It is there all the time, and if we give it time it will make itself known to us."
>
> Thomas Merton

Talk with God, or your higher power, who is kind and caring and would love to spend some time with you. Meet your guardian angel or angels, or a spiritual person who is there for you. Share with them and ask their advice.

Inner-Child Visuals

Talk with your inner child and re-parent her. Hold her and love her. Give her the time and nurturing that a young child needs. Let her know that you will keep her safe and protect her. Feel the peace that can come from this kind of an image.

This is an especially powerful way to use your guided imagery. If you are an abuse survivor or have other trauma in your childhood, write a different ending to your story—or write another story altogether.

See yourself visiting with family and close relations or friends if you wish. My father died when I was six, and when I was growing up I used to have long talks with him. I created my own visualizations.

Imagine a room with your parents, grandparents, and even your great-grandparents. Talk with each of them to find out their strengths and weaknesses. How are you like them? Find the positive ways they have influenced your life.

What if you didn't know them? How can you find out about them? Ask friends and family to give you information. Read their journals, if they kept them. Maybe there are other family members that kept journals or scrapbooks. Study them. Read about the political, cultural, and religious history of their day. Piece together your own understanding of who they were.

Self-Esteem Visualization

For a positive self-esteem visualization, imagine yourself in a scrapbook with pictures from your childhood. View each page and celebrate the good times of your life. Rewrite the negative times into positive ones.

Create an imagined safe house with life-sized pictures of you growing up. Place special mementos and favorite items in the house. Make it a calm, relaxing getaway just for you.

Worry

Sometimes it's hard to sleep at night because of worry. It's difficult to turn your mind off. Imagine a box next to your bed. When a thought comes into your head, put it in the box so you can think about it the next day. Write your fears on small pieces of paper and set them aside. The next day, you can decide if you really need to look at them and become anxious again.

Laugh

Laughing is one of the best ways to diffuse stress. Create a comedic visualization. Include funny stories from your friends. Read a joke book. Watch the comedy channel and visualize yourself as a part of it.

Create a Safe Place in Your Home

Fashion a safe place in your own home. I have a friend who lives continents away from her family, but she keeps a room with her grandmother's furniture and mementos. It is a safe place for her to go and connect with her loved ones now that she is so far away from home.

Include spiritual elements that work for you in your home decor.

I have pictures of my children and grandchildren in places where I can see them daily because they don't live close to me. Their portraits help me connect with them.

Other Techniques

Visualize yourself planting a flower garden, painting a beautiful picture, swimming in a stunning lake, going four-wheeling, or riding in a bike race.

Rewrite your fears, and create internal strength as you visualize. Face fears in visualizations by reducing others to miniature people.

Put up a shield against negativity around you. Then walk into positive light.

Maybe your visualization could be of a success you recently had that will inspire you toward more success. An artist friend loved to paint, but each time she sat down to work, she had a hard time putting the brush on the canvas. A critical voice in her head told her she wouldn't do a good job and that she had no creative ability. She seemed to be stuck. So before she began each painting she told herself that she was a good artist and she had creative ability. Then she thought back to the time when she finished her last painting, visualizing and feeling the success of that moment. These techniques helped her to start the next project.

Aromatherapy can also aid your process if you are interested.

Be as imaginative as you wish. Include creativity in all you do. It will cultivate your soul.

Deep Breathing

Breathing can help calm your anxiety and change nervous habits. Look at your actions and your mindset. Do you feel frustrated or anxious? Do you twist your hair or bite your fingernails? Stop the outside behavior and focus internally. Visualize calm and peace, and use your deep breathing to relax your body.

Begin the breathing process by cleansing your body with a deep inhalation. Breathe down into your lower abdomen. Visualize your breath going into your whole body. See it filling your legs and feet. Feel it fill your shoulders and arms down into your hands and fingers. Let it cleanse your body.

Breathe in through your nose and out through your mouth. Keep your chest still and allow your breath to fill your abdomen. This takes a little practice, but it is worth it.

Count to three as you breathe in and then again to three as you breathe out.

Don't allow yourself to be distracted. Stay focused on your breathing. Feel the power of release as you breathe out. For me, breathing releases pent-up anxiety, worry, and other negative emotions. It leaves me feeling liberated and cleansed.

This is a technique you can use any time, any place. You always have to breathe, so do it deeply while on the subway or driving your car or in a boring board meeting. When you find yourself feeling tense, start this breathing exercise, and it will release your negative emotions. This is an especially great exercise to do before bed.

Couple the breathing with a mantra that is healing for you. Use a message that is meaningful at this time of your life, such as this AA mantra:

> *"I am letting go of fear and filling my life with faith."*
> *Alcoholics Anonymous*

"I am" statements are powerful. Remember that you have to change the mind first, and then feelings and behavior will follow.

- I am sufficient.
- I am healthy.
- I am lovable.
- I have inner wisdom.
- I have the blessings of positive energy.

These statements will fill you with peace. If you have spiritual works that you read from, choose a statement of wisdom from there.

Let this be part of your healing program. Your life will last longer and you will be happier. My clients and I have found strength in making deep breathing part of a daily program.

Dreams

> *"Follow your heart and your dreams will come true."*
> *Proverb*

Some believe the higher self brings about spiritual dreams. When we see something in a dream, it becomes part of us. The ancients thought dreams predicted the future, and they attached prophetic significance to biblical dreams.

Dreams can provide interesting insights into your life. Keep a small notebook by your bed to write your dreams in when you awaken.

Clients who completed this exercise would ask me, "What does my dream signify?" I could have given them my educated guess as to the implication, but it would probably have had no meaning for them.

Practicing the Process

I would always turn the question back to them. "What do you think your dream indicates?" They would struggle to find the answer, but when they did venture a guess, the meaning became clear. Usually the dream turned out to be a metaphor about what was happening in their lives. They could look at their situation and choose to change it if they wished.

This is a wonderful way for you to access your inner wisdom and strengthen your understanding of self.

Sometimes you might have a recurring dream night after night. Look at the dream carefully. No two dreams are ever the same. In a field of daffodils, each one looks the same from a distance, but when examined closely, they all have individually defining characteristics. The smallest changes in your recurring dream may give you specific understanding.

Sometimes the place between waking and sleeping is a time to receive messages concerning your life. Listen. Your inner wisdom may be speaking to you during this relaxed time when the world will not interfere.

Use your dreams as an aid to self-understanding. Relate them to what is happening in your life and let your inner wisdom guide you in the interpretation.

Chapter 27

Inner Wisdom

We have the power within us to make decisions and find our own way. Sometimes it's difficult for us to look to ourselves for answers to our problems.

> *"We are all of God even as a little drop of water is of the ocean."*
> *Gandhi*

Tapping into your inner wisdom is a wonderful journey. How do you begin? Having the idea and then the goal are the first steps. Look inside yourself for understanding. When was the last time you used good judgment? Make a list. Ask a friend, a teacher, or a religious leader you admire to help you inventory your strengths. Let their love in and seek their caring. Talk things over with them.

Access Your Inner Guide

Find a comfortable place to be as you begin. Stay peaceful during this process. Peace invites light and knowledge to enter. Use your deep breathing and focus your thinking.

Call your wise one to mind. Make a picture of this person in your head. Be able to see them and describe them in detail. If you have a photograph, use that if you wish. List their attributes—their strengths and weaknesses.

Begin to build (or rebuild) a relationship with them. Say hello as you approach them, and let them respond. Invite them to be your inner guide. Tell them about your daily life, and listen to what they have to say in return.

Talk and share your problems. Pay attention to their advice. Evaluate what they have to say and look at all the options. Meet with them often.

I loved my father, and he loved me. We used to sit together and talk things over before he died. After his death, I continued to talk with him. He and I had long conversations and still enjoyed each other's company. He has continued to be with me throughout my life, just being there for me when I had problems or trouble in my life. Our relationship is different than if he had lived, but we have continued to be part of each other's lives even though his is gone. I know he loves me, and I certainly love him.

Let the love of your inner guide wash over you. Love and light fill us and heal us daily. Allow blessings of positive energy to bring love to you in abundance.

> "All we are is the results of what we have thought. The mind is everything. What we think we become."
>
> Buddha

Chapter 28

Gratitude

Gratitude is a powerful tool to get your mind going in a positive direction. Thinking and feeling grateful thoughts bring optimism and love. When positive energy flows, it eradicates anxiety and pride and takes you to a place of humility where you will be open to new ideas.

> *"Gratitude is not only the greatest of virtues, but the parent of all others."*
>
> *Cicero*

Keeping a gratitude journal brings positive energy. Emmons and McCullough, in the *Journal of Personality and Social Psychology*, studied counting blessings versus counting burdens and found those who focused on daily blessings were more optimistic, vigorous, pleasant, and better able to handle life's troubles. Their sleep improved and they were sick less often. They were more charitable and made greater progress toward their goals.

If these are all attributes you would like in your life, include gratitude in your day. There are as many ways to accomplish this as there are individuals. Find the way that works best for you.

Daily Gratitude Rituals

Detailed Gratitude Journal

A daily gratitude journal was useful for many of my clients. During the intense part of their healing, many of them kept detailed journals.

Depressed clients who kept a gratitude journal seemed able to let go of the depression sooner than those who did not write. When you focus on the positive, it enlightens the soul, which leads to more centering and affirmative thinking, which leads to more light. When you do this, a positive feedback loop has been established.

Include your gratitude in your regular daily journaling if you wish.

Daily Gratitude List

To keep yourself focused on positive thinking during the day, set a goal to list three blessings before you go to bed each night. At first it can be difficult to come up with three positive things you are grateful for. I have found this especially powerful when working with depression in children.

Calli, age seven, had a difficult time finding anything positive about herself. Thinking of three positive things to write down was overwhelming at first. In the beginning, her list included

- I am thankful for my hair.
- I am thankful to have my ballet class.
- I am thankful I finished my spelling.
- I am thankful I didn't yell at my sister.

As the weeks went by, her list changed:

- I am thankful for the new girl in school today.
- I am thankful for leaves. My dad and I raked them, and I jumped in them.
- I am thankful I know how to do my math.
- My mom and dad love me.

Calli's list began to include changes in her communication skills, her willingness to work hard, and her ability to allow the love of others into her life. And it all began with a gratitude list.

Daily Gratitude Thoughts

Adding one more task to your busy day can be overwhelming for some. But if you pair your daily gratitude thoughts with something else you do every day, it will add strength and light to your attitude. Your gratitude list may be said to yourself as you are driving in the car or riding on the subway. Or you could use your exercise time to complete a daily list of thankfulness.

If you can pair a task that you want to complete with one you always do, you have finished two tasks instead of one. I have a friend who would rather die than miss his daily golf game, so he says his gratitude mantras on the seventh hole, which has the most beautiful scenery. Now he never misses either one.

Gratitude Visualizations

I like to visualize, so at times I write gratitude visualizations out, but other times, I just take a few minutes and enjoy a moment in my mind.

I wonder at the magnificence of a rosebud unfolding. From its tiny tight enclosure, it bursts little by little into full bloom. Each petal plays a part in the whole. Color streaks through the softness from white to deep pink, from yellow to bright red. I am grateful for the individual beauty of every petal and the lovely flower they create together.

I am grateful for the mother robin that builds her nest on the ledge just outside my window. Soon tiny eggs appear, and then hungry baby birds. I am careful not to disturb them, but I watch the unfolding miracle of life. The mother teaches her young how to fly. She nudges them out of the nest, over and over again, until they take off. I wonder if the young ones are afraid as they begin the process of leaving the nest.

I love the memory of the touch of my grandmother's hand. I feel her closeness and know that she loves me. I was hers and she was mine. Some of her ways of thinking are my ways of thinking. Some of her habits are my habits. I feel connected to her, and I am thankful for her legacy.

I am grateful for the new life of a kitten or puppy. They frisk and romp and roll about. They pounce on a new toy or on a fellow creature. There is newness, innocence, and playfulness, a connecting with others that is refreshing.

Gratitude Mantras

All religions and great teachers find gratitude an important aspect of their teachings. When you see a quote you like, keep it in your mantra list. I have one on my computer that I consult daily. I love the wisdom they bring. Keep a new group of quotes on your desktop each week and say them every time you open your computer.

Here are some sample quotes on gratitude:

> *"When I admire the wonder of a sunset or the beauty of the moon, my soul expands in worship of the Creator."*
> — *Gandhi*

> *"We can walk through the darkest night with the radiant conviction that all things work together for the good."*
> — *Martin Luther King Jr.*

> *"Gratitude is the sign of noble souls."*
> — *Aesop*

> *"Gratitude is the fairest blossom which springs from the soul."*
> — *Henry Ward Beecher*

> *"Gratitude is the heart's memory."*
> — *Proverb*

> *"Thankfulness and appreciation are synonyms for gratitude."*
> — *Webster's Dictionary*

> *"A man's indebtedness . . . is not a virtue; his repayment is. Virtue begins when he dedicates himself actively to the job of gratitude."*
> — *Ruth Benedict*

I give thanks for myself and my divinity.

Trials Engender Gratitude

Unless you are very different from the rest of us, you have trials. We all have things in our lives that are difficult to handle. Look around your family and you will see them. Our niece's son has leukemia. Our daughter suffered loss in a divorce. A neighbor has Parkinson's disease.

Our trials can depress us and drag us down, or they can be a source of growth and maturity for us. Our niece has a sweet gentle personality, which is now coupled with strength and courage because of the medical difficulties she has experienced in dealing with the leukemia. Our daughter is raising two wonderful children. Her soul has been refined and polished through her divorce experience. Our dear neighbor finds joy in her life even with the Parkinson's disease. Some days she just endures the dizziness that comes from her medication; other days she can meet friends and enjoy their company. I can see the courage in her eyes as she gets herself out and about.

"You never miss the water until the well runs dry."

Proverb

Each time adversity becomes your companion, it brings you a gift. Treasure the gift and receive the wisdom that it brings. Take responsibility for the lesson, and put it into practice in your life. Let your higher power know of your gratitude.

Negative Energy and Gratitude

In order to release any negative energy you do not want, be able to look at it and identify it.

Welcome the negative energy as part of your life and look for the gift it brings.

Ask yourself what you would be if you let this energy go into the light.

Visualize yourself without this energy.

Are you confident enough to expose yourself in this way? If you can answer yes, visualize yourself releasing your pessimism into the light to be healed.

Be grateful you are not perfect. You are growing—filled with positive energy and light. You are in the process of becoming whole.

Keep a gratitude journal of your trials. It will be enlightening to go back and read the feelings you had when you were in your darkest hour.

You will see that you have walked into the light.

> *"Gratitude is confidence in life itself."*
>
> Robert Emmons

Gifts of Gratitude

Gifts of positive energy and light come abundantly to us if we are grateful. Gratitude washes the fog away from our vision so that we can see more clearly.

> *"Life is the first gift, love is the second, and understanding the third."*
>
> Marge Piercy

A terrible car accident killed a young father and child, leaving behind a wife and several children. The cause: a drunk driver. Situations like this are tragic and difficult for a family to experience. I was impressed by the attitude of the wife and mother. She knew it would be a difficult time for her family, but they would be blessed by God and strengthened as they drew near to Him. She seemed to recognize the refining fire as she faced this situation. She didn't engage in bitterness or vindictiveness or say life was unfair. Even though she had many difficult trials ahead, she accepted them with the knowledge that her family would be healed and strengthened.

> *"At every moment you are living and dying, coming further into life and going out of it."*
>
> Thomas Moore

Sometimes it's hard to feel grateful or look for the gifts. Remember, first we think, then feel, then act.

Think, Feel, Act

Even if you don't feel grateful, say the words. Then the feelings will come. There is a universal blessing that gratitude brings, and it will be yours if you just begin with words of thanks.

Chapter 29

Creating Gifts

Problems happen. Everyone's life has trials. Difficulties can either depress us or help us grow stronger. We can exist in daily lethargy, or we can allow wisdom to polish and refine our soul. It all depends on our attitude.

When we take responsibility for things that happen in life, we can change them. We can turn them into learning experiences and receive new light and positive blessings.

Taking personal accountability brings growth. If we do not take personal responsibility for the things that occur in our lives, then we are victims, being acted upon.

Taking Personal Responsibility

Virginia's son was killed in a car accident, and her daughter-in-law remarried. She wanted to keep in touch with her grandchildren but didn't know how. We brainstormed and these are a few of the ideas we came up with. She could keep in touch through

- Pictures
- Cards
- Letters
- Telephone calls

- Webcam
- Email
- Skype
- Videos
- Travel to visit them
- Bring them to her home for a visit

Technology is creating a smaller and smaller world, allowing us to connect with almost any place on our planet. Virginia was grateful for the blessings that come from living in this day and age. Several years ago she wouldn't have had so many options. Virginia took responsibility for her actions in this situation and made it work.

Being accountable creates a conduit for positive energy, which empowers. It gave Virginia freedom to find the gifts in her situation and solve her problems.

Express Your Feelings through Talents

Many clients I worked with were able to express their feelings through music, art, poetry, and dance. Some of them released their emotions during the dark days of their trials. Others who were abused as children released their hurt and anger through the creative arts when they became adults.

Angela had suffered severe abuse as a child. She grew into a strikingly beautiful woman with a lot of artistic ability. Through her drawing and painting, she released the shame of her childhood. One day she walked into my office with a large canvas pastel drawing of her abusive situation. It was a poignantly striking depiction of what she had experienced. At first she hid her artwork in a folder in my office, but as she healed she shared her drawings with others. I encouraged her to contact a local museum to display her paintings because she was an excellent artist, and she did.

I admire Angela greatly. It was a privilege for me to watch her inner wisdom refine her heart until it shone like pure gold.

Beauty feeds the soul. Let it shine forth in your life as is best for you.

Finding Gifts

People create gifts in a variety of ways. One little girl who had been abused found the gift of safety. She could protect herself by

- Being around people she trusted
- Screaming and running if she were in a dangerous situation
- Telling her parents if she had a problem
- Practicing letting her needs be known

> "Stop thinking of your dark nights as problems and begin to see them as opportunities for change."
>
> Thomas Moore

What about a gift in divorce? One man found his gift was freedom. He was not oppressed anymore. He also found the gift of autonomy and the gift of liberty in seeking a loving relationship, which led to personal strength.

I have a friend, Melissa, who stayed in a difficult marriage. At times she thought herself crazy not to leave, but her higher power and her inner guide helped her find success. The couple worked out their problems. The gifts she found were

- Making her needs known
- Standing up for herself
- Learning to negotiate
- Becoming more kind and loving

Her husband loves her and values her friendship now. They are happy and feel closer because their trials have refined them. As they grow old together, they are both grateful for the companionship they share.

We all have trials and problems. None of us will get through life without difficulties, and there are times when we feel in the depths of despair. That is not the time to look for the gift. Spend some time feeling the sorrow of your situation. Maybe you can find a friend that will just listen and not give advice. Take time to feel the pain; and *after* you have cried out your grief, begin to look for the gifts. Not before.

> "The harvest of old age is the recollection and abundance of blessings previously secured."
>
> *Cicero*

Live your life today so that you will have no regrets from this moment on. Choose your path, and make it a positive one. Add light to the world through an optimistic attitude, service, and love.

We have all made mistakes in the past and feel sorry for some of the things we have done. Ask forgiveness of those around you and present your past regrets to the healing power of light. Seek the gifts of light and love in every aspect of your life and you will find them.

We grow when we add gifts to the world and accept them as they come to us.

Remember the butterfly. It enters darkness before it emerges into light, beauty, and freedom.

Chapter 30

Write, Write, Write

Keeping a journal creates a window into your soul. As you write you will find hidden rooms and passageways you weren't aware of. Write to connect with yourself. Record your feelings, daily happenings, and aspirations. There are many ways to keep a journal. Use a pen and paper, a computer, your phone, a scrapbook, your blog, a tape recorder, or any other method that works for you.

> "The garden must be prepared in the soul first or else it will not flourish."
>
> *Proverb*

Keeping a Journal Is

A Time to Set Goals

Recording your goals in your journal is a wonderful way to keep track of them. It's a great way to check your progress and keep yourself on the path you wish to be on. As you look back you will see the strength you have gained and the development that has come to you over the years.

Not a Time to Record Everyday Mundane Tasks

My great-grandfather kept small, daily notebook journals. I am grateful to touch them and hold them because I know he wrote them, but they are filled with entries about buying hayseed, milking the cow, and mending fences. It is great to know what kind of activities filled his day, but I would have preferred to discover what was in his heart from his writing. He was a kind man, giving unselfishly to others in his community.

I would really like to connect with the desires, dreams, and hopes of his heart. I have to read between the lines to guess about his compassion and empathy for others. I wonder if he really knew himself, because he never really shared his feelings. You can't grow from your own writings if it's just about tasks and not about your perceptions.

Record daily tasks for posterity, but let your spirit shine forth in your writing. This will be a gift not only for your posterity, but also for yourself as you share your feelings.

A Time to Record Your Feelings

What a great way to discover what you are feeling and thinking. As I begin to write, my mindset is scattered and unfocused. But as I continue, the predicament I'm dealing with becomes clear. I feel free as I allow my feelings to spill onto the pages of my book. It's as if I have externalized the issue and can look at it more objectively.

As you work at this process, journaling will enrich your life. Read back over your record to see the maturity you have gained, the insight that has come to you, and the depth of feelings you possess.

A Time for Quiet

Stillness connects us with positive energy. It is a time to hear your inner wisdom, to know your wise teachers, to understand life. Solitude refreshes your spirit. Take some time to be alone and share your thoughts with yourself and your journal.

> "A man does not seek to see himself in running water, but in still water. For only what is itself still can impart stillness into others."
>
> Chuang-tse

A Time to Record Memories

Recollections recorded in your journal will refresh you many times over as you reread them. Your memories of the past will be richer because of your written record. Record a beautiful sunset colored blue and pink or orange and gold. Write about a field of daisies wafting in the wind, and it will be with you always.

A Time to Remember Your Senses

Write what you hear, smell, see, touch, taste. Include all your senses in your writing. They put you in touch with yourself.

> *"Nothing can cure the soul but the senses, just as nothing can cure the senses but the soul."*
>
> Oscar Wilde

A Time to Record Your Meditations

Keep a meditation journal. It will not only help you find focus and peace in your life, but will also be evidence of your growth as you rewrite and change your visualizations to fit your needs.

A Time to Record Your Vacations

Trips can be once-in-a-lifetime ventures. Record the places you see, the pictures you take, the feelings you have, the memories you make, and the people you meet. Use your blog to share these with your family. These entries will bring pleasure to you and your loved ones in years to come. As the years go by and your children and grandchildren visit some of your favorite places in the world, it will be fun to compare notes.

A Time to Dream

Keep a notebook by your bed to record your dreams. I forget mine if I don't write them down immediately. Write your interpretations in your dream journal. I like to keep a separate record of dreams because it usually takes me a few days to think about them and decipher their meaning. Dream interpretation connects you with your subconscious.

A Time to Record Your Gratitude

Keep a separate gratitude journal if you wish. It will be a blessing in your life for years to come.

> "Keep a grateful journal. Every night, list five things that happen this day that you are grateful for. What it will begin to do is change your perspective of your day and your life."
>
> *Oprah Winfrey*

Creative Journals

Remember that creating beautiful art can release pent-up feelings during the healing process. Some of the clients I worked with made separate journals of their art, poetry, and creative writing.

Carol enjoyed sewing. She created quilt blocks and made them into wonderful coverlets as her healing journal. Her mother sewed when Carol was a child, so Carol had material scraps from all her childhood clothes. Carol made a party quilt from all her fancy dresses, a Sunday quilt out of her church clothes, and an everyday quilt using her play clothes. She displayed them at a church dinner one night. They were amazing. She said she could feel her inner child grow in strength as the child watched (and helped) Carol sew. Her inner child knew Carol really listened and cared.

Cynthia Rylant understood this concept when she wrote *Missing May*. May created wind chimes the way Carol sewed quilts. May left her legacy in the wind chimes after she was gone; Carol created her legacy in her quilts.

Inner-Child Journal

Allow your inner child (the little girl you used to be) to fashion a journal of her own. It is a very effective tool for connecting with your past. Let the child create it just as she wishes. If you use your nondominant hand, your child will speak to you with drawings or writings or maybe a new creation.

Connect with your inner child by asking questions. Use your dominant hand as the adult and your nondominant hand as the child. With your right hand (if you are right-handed) ask your inner child questions like

- How old are you?
- What is your name?

- How do you feel?
- Are you happy or sad?
- Are you scared?

Allow the child to respond to each question as you ask it by using your left hand (if you are right-handed) to write the answer. She will tell you what she is thinking and how she feels. Be patient with her as she struggles to record her answer with her kindergarten scrawl.

Inner-child journaling is an insightful way to begin to know yourself and listen to your feelings.

Roxanne grew up in a household where her parents were perfectionists. They were critical of her in all she did. She tried to be perfect, but she never quite measured up. She became demanding and critical as an adult—just like her parents.

I asked her to write a meditation to get acquainted with her inner child. She wrote a very nice visualization where she held the six-year-old Roxanne and told her she loved her. Even though she used the meditation several times, she said she didn't feel a connection. Usually that kind of exercise will bring emotions rushing to the surface.

Since Roxanne felt no link with her inner child, she used the journaling technique to ask little Roxanne how she felt. Little Roxanne told her she was afraid of her. She was scared Roxanne would be mean to her like her mom and dad were.

Roxanne worked for several weeks with the questioning method to gain her inner child's trust. Soon Roxanne was able to comfort and love the little girl that she was, because little Roxanne came to trust her.

Privacy

Safety is important to many people. Some of my clients worried about their children reading their journals. Others were concerned about ex-husbands finding them. If you are concerned, hide your journal. If you work on a computer, lock it with a password.

Healing and positive thinking brings trust and hope into our lives. As time goes along, you will be able to slip your journal in your desk without worry, but until that time comes, protect yourself.

Journaling Groups

You may be interested in finding a journaling group or creating one yourself. Find a group of women who are interested in journaling like you are. You can sit together and write once a month, share your writing with each other, and talk about how the journaling process has helped you.

Check with your community college writing classes, your church, or your local bookstore to see if one has already been established. If not, find a group of friends and establish your own.

It is important for the group to set rules of safety and privacy and to decide how the organization will function in general. Where will you meet? How often? Will you have refreshments?

Since you want the group to be a positive experience, allow only caring, nurturing feedback from members. If a member of a group has a problem, it needs to be addressed with the entire group in a positive way—not by side-talking with other members.

Remember, groups could be established for any kind of journaling, including scrapbooking and blogging.

A group experience is a wonderful way to meet your goals and a great way to establish lasting friendships. Enjoy one another's company.

Chapter 31

Thought Stopping and Thought Substitution

Because our thinking determines our feelings and then our actions, it's important to keep our thinking going in a positive direction. If you have been through a devastating experience, you know it can be difficult to find a place in your mind for optimism.

Thought stopping means to cease thinking about a negative subject. When you find yourself focusing on a topic you wish to eradicate, say "STOP" in your head. If you are alone, say it out loud. This action immediately centers your thinking on the "STOP."

As you say "STOP," picture a STOP sign in your head. You have then interrupted your thinking with both a verbal command and a picture.

Thought substitution is a term used to mean just what it says. Find an alternative subject to think about. Preferably, consider an issue that is positive and something you enjoy, like a hobby, a wise mantra, a family member, or anything you choose.

> "There is a technique, a knack, for thinking, just as there is for doing other things. You are not wholly at the mercy of your thoughts, any more than they are you. They are a machine you can learn to operate."
>
> *Alfred North Whitehead*

Stinking Thinking

"All that we are is the result of what we have thought. The mind is everything. What we think we become."

Buddha

I had some clients that suffered the pains for divorce and couldn't let go of the relationship. They wondered from moment to moment what their ex-spouse was doing—sure that he was having a wonderful time in a new relationship.

Thought stopping and thought substitution day by day is the best way out of this dilemma. Studying the words of a great teacher and writing some mantras the like following ones also help.

"We are shaped by our thoughts; we become what we think. When the mind is pure, joy follows like a shadow that never leaves."

Buddha

"Do not let what you cannot do interfere with what you can do."

John Wooden

"Change your thoughts and you change your world."

Norman Vincent Peale

"But hushed be every thought that springs / From out the bitterness of things."

William Wordsworth

"Success: Peace of mind which is a direct result of self-satisfaction in knowing that you did your best to become the best that you are capable of becoming."

John Wooden

Attracting Negativity with Your Thoughts

I had several clients who focused on the minute details of their health problems. They were so centered on their shortcomings that their problems became worse.

If this is your situation, changing your thinking to positive attributes concerning your health will be helpful. Write about the miracles of your life. Your eyes are such intricate creations. Man cannot duplicate their ability to see, even with the most expensive camera. Your lungs help you breathe. Your heart keeps your blood pumping. These parts of you are achievements greater than any man can produce. You are a miracle.

"All the events in your life are a mirror image of your thought."
Mark Fisher

Use thought stopping and thought substitution to find a positive path. As you allow light into your life, enjoy the blessings optimistic thinking brings.

Chapter 32

Becoming New

Positive energy is all around you. It is the essence of spring and the fruit of summer. It is the flutter of fall leaves and the fairyland of a winter snow. It comes each day with the rising of the sun and enters night with the beauty of the starry moon-filled sky. Look around you; it is in all you behold. Include it in your thinking and your life.

Perception

Our perception of a situation drives our thinking and feeling. We all see the world a little differently. The following is an example of how two people looked at an event, each in their own way.

Felicity and Ingrid received an invitation to a weekend workshop on goal setting. The boss told them the company would pay all expenses.

Felicity wondered if her boss was considering her for a promotion and she was excited. Why would the company go to the expense of sending her to the workshop if she were not in line to move up the corporate ladder?

Ingrid worried about the workshop. She thought the boss would only send her to the workshop because her skills were insufficient. Maybe she would be fired if she didn't complete work well enough. Why would the boss single her out unless she could see that Ingrid was inadequate?

Anxiety and stress trigger our perceptions—not external events themselves. If we choose to look at things that happen in a positive way, we see upcoming events as wonderful. If we look at the negative, things seem insurmountable.

A positive outlook engenders optimism. Felicity was excited about the workshop and knew a promotion would be hers. Picture the way Felicity would present herself at the workshop. The positive message she sent out would come back her way.

> *"The greatest discovery of my generation is that human beings can alter their lives by altering their attitudes of mind."*
>
> William James

If we are negative, we feel trapped in double binds, with no way to win. Ingrid believed the boss was punishing her by sending her to the workshop. She began many of her worry sentences with "What if," causing herself much stress and anxiety. She put herself in a double bind by thinking, "If I go to the workshop, the boss will see that I believe I am disorganized and incompetent. If I don't go to the workshop, the boss will see me as uncooperative and unwilling to follow orders."

How do you think Ingrid presented herself at the workshop? Her message to the world engendered negativity that would come back her way.

Reframing our views from negative to positive is a matter of thinking modification. Belief influences our behavior and our stress. Stop and think thoughts that are positive and solution focused.

> *"You might well remember that nothing can bring you success but yourself."*
>
> Napoleon Hill

Rewriting Your Story

Everyone has a way of thinking that they learned during childhood. They tell these stories to themselves over and over until they become their only reality. It might be a story of a happy childhood or a tale of abuse and confinement or even one of battling for independence. This idea about the world affects their life in a positive or negative way. Rewrite your story and it will alter your perception of life.

Here is my narrative:

My great-grandfather on my mother's side was hit in the head by a heavy piece of equipment when my grandmother was a girl. He didn't live a long life. My grandfather died of typhoid fever when my mother was six. An angry teenager ran a stop sign and killed my father in a car wreck when I was six.

My story became "Men abandon me." I worried each time one of our children turned six that my husband would die. He didn't.

I lived my life as if the men in my existence were going to abandon me. This was a subconscious belief that I didn't voice, but it was there. As I came to understand my story, I decided to rewrite it:

- Men are supportive of me.
- The men in my life stay with me.
- The men in my life care for me.
- I am loved.
- I am cherished.

The positive reframe uplifted me. As I said my mantras over and over, my thinking began to change. I opened myself up to the love others wanted to give me. I quit living my life as if I had to cling to men or they would leave me. I could allow my husband to be himself, and I could be myself. I was now free in my relationships.

What is your story? Did you learn to watch your back or can you trust others? Did you run away as a solution to your problems, or did your learn to stay and fight it out? Were problems hidden and never discussed or were they solved by talking? Did you belong to a fighting family where you had to argue to make your point? Did significant family members escape daily life by seeking an addiction? Did you learn to run and hide? Are you still doing it?

The list is endless because no two families are exactly the same. No one has a story that is just like yours. Write your story down and change it as you would like.

A New Vision

Picture your ideal self with your new perception of life. Now take your ideal self with your new perception of life and write a new story. Take the information you wrote about your best self and rewrite who you are becoming, including your change in perception and story.

Now that you have described the person you are to become, set your goals from the details you have just fleshed out.

- Visualize the person you want to become.
- Develop goals to become this person.
- Write mantras to program your brain to believe your best self.
- Imagine your best self saying these phrases as part of your meditation.

> "Imagination is everything. It is the preview of life's coming attractions."
>
> Albert Einstein

The mind-body connection is great. Use your positive energy to aid you in your pursuit of your goals. Visualize yourself as successful with positive light and energy. Let the mind-body connection work for you in a proactive way. Your effort will help you achieve your goals. Perceive yourself as successful and you will be.

Your Body Will Believe Your Mind

The mind is able to change the body in many ways. Those who have suffered physical illness know that positive thinking helps heal the body as well as the mind.

We had a dear friend diagnosed with terminal cancer. Determined to get well, she used guided imagery each day to see herself as well and whole. She imagined her body believing her mind. She worked with the doctors and took advantage of the latest methods and procedures. Immersing herself in positive energy—surrounding herself with good friends, light, and love—became the focus of each day.

We moved, and I didn't see her for a while, but I ran into her in a social setting a couple of years later. She had several of her grandchildren with her. Her cancer was in remission, and she felt great physically.

Her positive thinking had helped heal her. Her mind had blessed her body with health.

"Your real boss is the one who walks around under your hat."
Napoleon Hill

Positive Energy

Fill yourself with light and love. Let yourself be part of the luminosity. Add to the brightness. Whatever your passion is, fulfill it. Become your best self. Make the world a better place with one small thought at a time.

Chapter 33

Desensitization

Many people have phobias or anxieties, including
- Fear of flying
- Fear of snakes
- Fear of certain animals
- Fear of enclosed places, like elevators
- Fear of driving on busy roads
- Fear of germs
- Fear of certain foods

The list could go on and on. The reasons for eliminating these anxieties are because they keep you in a state of heightened fear, and they alter your lifestyle so you aren't free to live as you would like.

"Fear is false expectations appearing real."

Unknown

The process of desensitizing yourself to the false expectations that appear real is called systematic desensitization. After learning to relax, this is a process of exposing yourself to the fearful situation gradually so that you remain peaceful and become desensitized to it. You learn, through this method, to cope with the situation so that it doesn't alter your lifestyle.

Survival Strategies

Learning to cope with anxiety is an important skill to master before you expose yourself to a fearful situation. Calming techniques such as relaxing your muscles and body parts, meditation, positive visualization, and deep breathing are all useful.

Imagining positive outcomes of your anxiety-laden situation turns your mind in a new direction, just as rewriting a bad dream with a good ending reduces fear and calms shaky nerves.

For many people, the combination of medication plus behavior modification works well. If you have anxiety, check with your medical doctor or a psychiatrist to see if medication is an option you want to explore.

Establishing a Hierarchy

After learning to relax yourself, the next step is to expose yourself to the fearful situation a little bit at a time. I've outlined the entire process here, and examples to clarify will follow.

Use the following method:
- Brainstorm all possible exposure to your fearful situation.
- Create ten to twenty incidents.
- Write them on cards or separate pieces of paper.
- Reduce the number to about fifteen.
- Order each incident from the least fearful to the most fearful.
- Set a specific time for meditation (a time to focus) on each anxiety-producing task that you can pair with a relaxation technique you have chosen. Decide whether you will do this daily, three times a week, or once a week.
- Focus on the imagined situation for several seconds. The amount of time can vary according to the amount of anxiety each situation creates. If an image calls up a great amount of fear, focus on it for only a few seconds.
- Use calming techniques to keep yourself relaxed as you focus on each incident.

Exposing Yourself to Fear

There are two ways to introduce yourself to the fearful situations: you can write down your imagined examples and visualize them, or you can expose yourself to real situations.

Imagined Fear

This type of fear is called "in vitro," or artificial. It is a very effective technique to start out with because the brain can't tell if something is real or imagined. Pairing imagined situations with peacefulness can be helpful at first to defuse the emotions.

Real Fear

This type of fear is referred to as "in vivo," or live threats. To completely conquer a fear, it is necessary to expose yourself to these situations. For instance, the last item on your desensitization list may be to take an airplane flight, visit a zoo to watch the snakes being fed, or ride an elevator.

Life-Altering Fear

Blair was afraid to drive on the busy streets of the large western city she lived in. It was difficult for her to get to work each day because she had to avoid all the main intersections. She spent at least an hour going to and from work when the trip could have taken fifteen minutes.

Blair began her desensitization process by brainstorming a list of scenes. She ordered them according to the anxiety they produced in her.

Her list included a picture of

- a busy street from the newspaper
- a policeman writing a traffic citation
- a pedestrian at the intersection of a busy street
- a passenger in a car on the busy street
- herself driving on a moderately busy street
- herself driving on a busy street
- Blair standing on the corner of a busy street
- Blair sitting in a car parked at the side of a busy street
- Blair riding as a passenger in a car on the busy street

- Blair driving her car on a moderately busy street
- Blair driving her car on a busy street

Blair practiced her relaxation techniques. Meditation and deep breathing were the ones she used the most. She decided to do the desensitization process twice a week. She worked with three items each time. Then when she began the next session, she would always start with the last item she had worked with the time before. If she still had anxiety over an item, she practiced relaxing with it for several sessions.

It took about six weeks before Blair could drive to work on busier roads, and she still avoided rush-hour traffic. Driving on busy roads was never something she enjoyed, but it didn't hinder her life like it had before. She was relieved to have the positive energy in her life, and she was grateful for the strength she gained from the process.

If you have anxieties, work to create a lifestyle that is inclusive rather than exclusive. It will be a tremendous boost to your self-esteem to be in control of your life, rather than being trapped in fear.

"In a calm sea every man is a pilot."

John Ray

# Chapter 34

Laughter

Laughter is the best medicine. What more can be said? This old adage is true for all of us. A little senselessness keeps you stress free and perpetuates a healthy mind.

> *"Laughter translates into any language."*
>
> Roy Zuck

Humor Can Erase Negativity

Jillian disliked her husband Russell's criticism of her and their children. It seemed he was always telling her what to do, assuming that she and the kids weren't good enough. Jillian told Russell she didn't like him interfering all the time, but nothing changed.

One day when Russell was in the middle of a lecture concerning the "correct" way to stack the dishes in the dishwasher, Jillian said, "Fish."

"Fish?" Russell said. "What does that have to do with our discussion?"

"Nothing," Jillian said, and she began to laugh.

Russell looked at her and smiled. "I'm being critical again, aren't I?"

They both laughed. After that, the word "fish" became a code word that either of them could say when they found themselves repeating the pattern.

> "Humor is a prelude to faith and laughter is the beginning of prayer."
>
> Reinhold Niebuhr

Children and Humor

Children are wonderful instruments of humor. I was in a meeting once where a little boy took off his shoe and twirled it around his head by the laces, then let it fly. It sailed into an older lady's lap. She began to giggle and soon had everyone laughing.

My little granddaughter was excited when I came to visit her in Portland, Oregon. She wanted to show me the sights, and when we saw Mt. Hood in the distance, and she turned to me and said, "Look, Grandma, there is Mountain Hood."

Our nephew insisted on calling my husband "Uncle Bog" instead of "Uncle Bob."

My brother wanted to shave when he was in second grade, so he cut off his eyebrows. He looked just like a ghost.

A young mother and her son each took a spray can of whipped cream to the backyard and had a cream fight before they ran through the sprinklers.

Every family has a story of a toddler smearing lipstick all over his face or a preschooler dumping baby powder on another child until they both look like ghosts. Maybe the grade school kids had a mud fight in the back yard. Find your own funny anecdotes and have a good laugh at your next family party.

> "I would not exchange the laughter of my heart for the fortunes of the multitudes."
>
> Kahlil Gibran

Positive Energy

> "Those who do not know how to weep with their whole heart, don't know how to laugh either."
>
> Golda Meir

Passion and feeling come from the heart. There is a time for both laughter and crying. After the tears, make laughter part of your life.

Let your hilarity be only positive. Silly movies, comedy shows, and funny memories are all wholesome and healthy. Keep the positive energy flowing with your mirth.

Amusement reduces stress and allows free flow of positive energy into your life. Let laughter keep your conduit open to giving and receiving.

Chapter 35

Communication: Listening and Reflecting

"We begin from the recognition that all beings cherish happiness and do not want suffering. It then becomes both morally wrong and pragmatically unwise to pursue only one's own happiness oblivious to the feelings and aspirations of all others who surround us as members of the same human family. The wiser course is to think of others when pursuing our own happiness."

The Dalai Lama

One of the ways we think of others is in our communication methods. We are in touch with others through our nonverbal cues, and by the words we speak. Sometimes just a glance toward a loved one lets them know how we feel.

Communications Patterns

If you have a problem to discuss with your partner or a friend, how do you handle it? What kind of communication skills do you have? How would you assess them?

Do you ignore a problem until you get angry and then attack? Do you beat around the bush when you have something difficult to discuss? Do you confront the person or problem head-on? Are you brutally honest in your assessment of a situation? Have you read enough communication books to be politically correct when using phrases like, "I feel ___ about ___ because ___"?

Your feelings determine the way you handle communication problems. If you ignore difficulties or beat around the bush, maybe it's because you're afraid to hurt someone. You may be afraid the other person will not like you if you are honest with them. Or maybe you really don't know how you feel.

When you hold feelings inside and do not address a problem, irritation, frustration, and then anger build. Finally you explode when the pressure becomes too strong to bear. I saw this communication pattern recur over and over with couples in therapy. If you are irritated, address the problem early, and it will probably be worked out through a rational discussion. If the issue is left to fester, it can be blown out of proportion. Then it becomes larger than necessary.

If you don't address a problem with your partner, you are protecting yourself and the other person from change, and that keeps the relationship stuck. When you say nothing, you are doing a tremendous disservice to both you and the other person. You aren't honoring yourself enough to let your wants and needs be known. Your partner doesn't know how others see him until he is told. He can't change if no one gives him feedback. People can't modify their behavior if they don't know how others feel.

Have you ever been around someone who wants to tell you something but doesn't have the courage? You know they want to say something, and you can almost guess what it is, but they don't say anything. It's an uncomfortable feeling for me. I would rather have an honest discussion with someone about what they want to tell me, even if it is negative.

It takes courage to talk about a problem. Before I became a therapist, I was afraid of clear communication. I am much better now, and our family is healthier in the ways we relate to each other because we talk and share our feelings. If one person changes, it creates a difference in the entire group. It's like dropping a pebble in the middle of a still pond. The ripples wave across the water, reaching every edge.

People might be afraid of you if you come on too strong by attacking and blaming. Others may discount what you say if you are not sensitive to their feelings. This kind of communication is a sure recipe for a fight. There is anger, pride, and criticalness associated with this type of communication. If this is your pattern, look inside yourself. Where is your compassion? Is fear covering it?

Anger is a blanket of protection for your fear.

Vocabulary of Communication

If you are to be credible in your communication, you must consider the other person and their feelings. Couples get into fights because they are critical and attack each other. How can you share your true thoughts without attacking?

If you use "I feel ___ about ___ because ___," you have to think before you talk.

Own your feelings, and own your communication. If you can't stand a messy toothpaste tube because it's been squeezed in the middle, don't say, "I hate it when you squeeze the toothpaste tube in the middle. You are so messy." Try instead, "I am frustrated when the toothpaste tube is squeezed in the middle because it's so messy."

"I feel irritated about the dirty dishes in the kitchen sink because the food gets dried on when they aren't rinsed and put in the dishwasher." Figure out a way to take turns or work together to clean up dinner.

"I feel upset about the mud tracked in on the kitchen floor because I don't want to clean it up." A natural consequence for getting mud on the floor is to have the person with the muddy shoes clean it up themselves. Work out a plan together.

Own your feelings. It keeps you from attacking and blaming. If you keep the "you" statements out of the discussion, and focus on the "I" statements, the message is much softer.

Write out your statements if you have trouble finding the words. It will give you time to sort out your feelings.

The phrase of "I feel ___ about ___ because ___" is only a starting place. Use it until you have developed enough skill to branch out with other words. It may sound rehearsed—memorized. It is. Learn to really talk to your partner, share your feelings, and listen.

Relationship Mirrors

Talking with another person is like holding up a mirror for yourself. Watch the communication patterns of others and see if you can discover how they feel inside. Someone that talks incessantly probably feels anxiety and fear inside. A person who is critical of others usually has anger bottled up inside them.

Relationships are like mirrors. As you talk about others you will see yourself in what you say.

An example would be, "I hate it when you are so critical of me. You attack me all the time." If the person talking holds up the mirror, she will see that she is the one being critical—not the person being blamed.

A positive example would be, "I feel uncomfortable when you are critical of me. It hurts my feelings." This person has taken time to assess her feelings and share in a nonthreatening way.

If you have a problem with communication, take time to know your own feelings about a situation. Journal or talk with a friend until you can converse in a clear and kind manner. Ask your partner to listen while you share your feelings.

Be insightful and caring for yourself as well as your partner. Listen to yourself as well as your partner.

> *"We flatter those we scarcely know, we please the fleeting guest, and deal full many thoughtless blow to those who love us best."*
>
> Ella Wheeler Wilcox

Listening to Others

Listening does not mean being quiet so you can get your rebuttal ready while the other person is talking. You have to listen carefully enough to your partner explain his feelings that you can repeat them back. Keep reflecting until your partner is satisfied that you understand.

Then you can say your feelings. Allow your partner to listen and reflect your feelings until you are satisfied that he has really heard you.

Share your dreams and your hopes, your aspirations and your goals. Listen to your partner's desires and wishes.

Practicing the Process

This process of communicating is intimate because you really come to know each other as you engage in it. To know another person is to connect with a divine creation. What a privilege! Allow it to work in your life. As you give to others by sharing and listening, they will begin to do the same. Give and receive in abundance!

"I never knew how to worship until I knew how to love."
Henry Ward Beecher

Listening to Ourselves

Because we are all imperfect and have problems, it is important for us to listen to ourselves. Do you really listen to what's going on inside you, or are you just reacting to outside stimuli? Through our actions, we teach others how to treat us. How do you teach others to treat you?

"We come to love not by finding a perfect person, but by learning to see an imperfect person perfectly."
Sam Keen

"Every man is a divinity in disguise, a God playing the fool."
Ralph Waldo Emerson

Terry was depressed. She could find the negative in any situation given. I asked her what were the benefits depression and negativity brought her. At first Terry couldn't come up with anything. After she thought about it, she said she had great compassion for others because she suffered. In attending to this process, Terry began to change her negative thinking patterns into solution-focused ones. She still had optimistic thinking to develop, but she could see the good in herself and be grateful for her gifts of humanness.

"When left unhealed, the past will destroy our lives. It buries our unique gifts, our creativity, and our talents."
Unknown

There is wisdom in listening to ourselves and finding all the gifts we have been given. I am grateful for the human gifts that are mine. I have to work with them and modify myself, but I am grateful for this process because I gain wisdom and strength in the process.

"When we love—we grow."
Gautier

Chapter 36

Accountability Groups

Talking with others or being involved with a group is a wonderful way to make friends and become connected. You could go walking with a friend early in the morning, meet someone at the gym during lunch, or enjoy a dinner meeting with companions. Be flexible in setting up what works for you.

The buddy system or accountability group is good for lots of reasons:
- Sociality is great.
- It gives you a time to share and keeps you defined and focused.
- You have a place of accountability.
- Positive reinforcement of your work is a motivator.
- Creativity can be fostered.
- Brainstorming ideas helps you think outside the box.
- It's just plain fun to get together.

Meeting with friends is a wonderful way to make yourself accountable for your goals. As we work with others, we find ourselves following through on our commitments to ourselves.

Set a time that works for you—whatever you and your friends find best. Your group can be formally organized or unstructured, as you wish.

Guidelines for Getting Started

- Decide a meeting time and place. Be flexible, but consistent.
- Establish guidelines that work for group members.
- Give only positive suggestions and compliments.
- You might begin each meeting by going around the circle and giving everyone a sincere compliment concerning her goals.
- Give everyone a chance to account for her progress in a positive way.
- No negatives are to be spoken, either in the person's progress report or in the input from others. Put each suggestion in positive terms.
- Brainstorm creative ways to remember your goals each day—like keeping a penny in your shoe to remind you of your goal or giving yourself a jellybean every time you accomplish an objective.
- Create and share gratitude statements concerning your goals.
- Ask for feedback in writing mantras that will change your thinking.
- Construct positive statements about achieving your goals.
- Give everyone in your group a hug if they would like one.

Group Rules

Many of the ideas in the previous section can be incorporated into the rules you would like to establish in your group. I have seen groups function in a variety of different ways, from structured to flexible, and from very focused to more casual.

Please remember: No negativity is to be allowed in the group—no negative side-talking about other members, no negative self-talk, no negative feedback to group members. Whatever needs to be said can be done in a positive way.

Group Decisions

Often, groups need to make decisions. If the meeting place needs to be changed or a new time would work better for some, let the decisions for change be a group effort. When some of the members may need to be absent from the group, let the group as a whole decide how to handle the situation.

For instance, if the host or hostess of the group will be out of town at the prescribed meeting time, the group could decide
- To meet in an alternate place
- To reschedule when everyone can be present
- To cancel that meeting

Group decisions voted on by the majority of the members will fit the needs of the group and keep the power centered and balanced among members.

Group Synergism

Groups that meet together can develop a synergism that can benefit all of their members. If light and optimism are present, everyone benefits.

When mules pulled borax out of Death Valley in the late 1800s, it is said that the workers tried different combinations of mule trains to pull the borax. Their goal was to get the greatest amount of borax out with the fewest mules. They found that a twenty-mule team could pull more borax out of the mines than any other combination of mules. The synergism of twenty mules working together was greater than the sum of the separate parts.

Groups can be the same way. The love, ideas, and support that come from a group can be greater than the individual parts. As the group works together, ideas shared lead to more ideas. Support engenders greater support.

The following are statements your group might adopt as a mantra to discuss or be recited at the beginning of each meeting.

"Goals that are not written down are just wishes."

Dodson

> "If you're bored with life—you don't get up every morning with a burning desire to do things—you don't have enough goals."
>
> Lou Holtz

> "Confusion of goals and perfection of means seem—in my opinion—to characterize our age."
>
> Albert Einstein

> "Obstacles are those frightful things you see when you take your eyes off your goal."
>
> Henry Ford

Chapter 37

What Successful People Have

What does success mean? If we were to ask fifty people, we would probably get fifty different answers. Is it wealth? Is it fame? Does it mean being a great teacher or writer or artist?

It could be any or all or none of these things. Webster's dictionary defines success as "the favorable or prosperous termination of attempts or endeavors." I like this explanation because it includes all people in all walks and pursuits of life.

I have an aunt who works in her garden every day. Her lawn and flowerbeds resemble a park. She isn't famous or wealthy, but she is successful at what she loves in life. We have a friend down the street who loves to visit the sick. Every day she is at the assisted living residence or someone's bedside to cheer them up. She will never be well known or rich, but she is happy and enjoying her existence. Both these women are living the abundant life they have chosen. The world has blessed them, and they receive as they give.

I have found that most successful people have common characteristics. Now, granted, I have not done a scientific study on successful people, nor have I met all the successful people in the world. The following are only observations of my own. Use them, as they are helpful for you.

Virtues

Steady Temperament

People that have a steady temperament are constant in their disposition. They learn to share their feelings while remaining firm in their character. Those who work to develop a balanced temperament have the added blessing of knowing their feelings and being able to share them while remaining stable.

> "Only a man's character is the real criterion of worth."
> — Eleanor Roosevelt

Self-Discipline

Success is difficult if one does not have discipline. Procrastination and a poor work ethic hamper many talented individuals in their chosen field of endeavor. Set goals and work toward them. Little, individual steps create permanent change. Feel the excitement as you begin to see internal changes in yourself. Change comes for all of us one step at a time.

Sense of Values

The world is much more mobile than it used to be. We are able to connect with others around the world who have different viewpoints. I have a dear Muslim friend whom I admire. We visited while our children played at the park. When we lived in California, we had Jewish neighbors. Our holiday meals together included a Seder dinner. Both these friends and their children have become very successful in their chosen endeavors in life. Each family has its own sense of values, and the children know what their family believes and stands for. Identify your sense of values, share them with your family, and live them.

> "Your habits become your values. Your values become your destiny."
> — Gandhi

Solution-Focused Attitude

Life is full of obstacles and challenges. We can either complain about our situation, or we can take responsibility for ourselves and find a solution. Create a door in the wall if there is no way through. Brainstorm possible answers to a problem and then choose a solution.

> "Focus ninety percent of your time on solutions and only ten percent of your time on problems."
>
> Anthony J. D'Angelo

Ability to Embrace Change

Have there been times in your life when you were resistant to change? Sometimes change takes a while to get used to. I had a friend who used to say to her children, "The train is pulling out of the station and you can either get on it or get left behind."

> "God grant me the serenity to accept the things I cannot change, courage to change the things I can, and wisdom to know the difference."
>
> Alcoholics Anonymous

A Sense of Humor

Laughter is a great gift. It is grounding when life seems overwhelming. It gives you a perspective on life. Your mood will be much steadier if you include humor in your life to relieve your stress.

I watch my favorite British comedy before bed. It's like taking a sleeping pill for me. I rest well and am refreshed the next day.

I have a doctor friend who recommends laughter for his cancer patients. He feels it aids their healing.

> "Every survival kit should include a sense of humor."
>
> Unknown

Tools for Healthy Living

Leisure Time

Everyone needs some time to recreate. Do your "thing," whatever that is. Sometimes we get so busy that we don't take time for ourselves to do what we love. When you aren't taking care of yourself, your body will tell you. When it happens to me, I either get a cold or have back problems. Both of these ailments send me to my bed so I can read a good novel. By the time the novel is finished, I am better. I have learned to skip the sickness part and just read for fun.

Find a hobby, like skiing, skating, gardening, or anything you wish. Being out in nature or having your hands in the soil can be nurturing. Discover what works for you and let your passion free.

> *"If bread is the first necessity of life, recreation is a close second."*
> Edward Bellamy

A Support System

Successful people have a good support system. It could be a self-help group or a collection of people who enjoy a hobby. Our nephew enjoys mountain biking. He joined a bike club and loves it. It might also be a church group or a sewing club. My husband and I had a friend who loved to cross-stitch. He learned the skill from his mother as a boy. He met with the ladies in the sewing club one evening a week and had a great time. Think outside the box.

Many times, blessings of positive energy come through those around us in the form of wisdom and advice and just love. You need a minimum of four hugs per day. Be sure you give them and ask for them.

> *"Friends are the flowers in life's garden."*
> Unknown

Healthy Eating and Sleeping Habits

Self-care skills, like eating and sleeping, need to be at the top of your list. If you are depressed or anxious, you are probably not eating or sleeping well. Both are prerequisites to being healthy. None of us function well if we do not care for our bodies.

If you have physical problems, check with a doctor about the symptoms and solutions. Set a nutritional program for yourself that will meet your needs. There are so many good plans. Happy reading in this area!

Exercise

This is a vital area. Get your heart rate up, or just enjoy a walk through the park or neighborhood.

I have a friend who jogs with friends daily. One of the joggers, Salinda, has terminal cancer. It is still in the early stages, so she can still exercise. She loves life and takes one day at a time. Salinda's positive attitude is infectious. Everyone benefits from it.

Combine several goals together if you wish. You can find a support group that exercises, like the bike club. Find what works for you and commit several hours a week. Feel wonderful because of it.

> *"Those who do not find time for exercise will have to find time for illness."*
>
> *Proverb*

Expand Your Vision

There is a bird feeder in our backyard filled with a mixture of wild birdseed. The smaller birds prefer the little seeds and drop the sunflower seeds on the ground because they are so big.

A little squirrel comes to eat the sunflower seeds left by the little birds. He was enjoying a feast one evening when a dove landed near him. The dove raised its wings to frighten the squirrel, but the squirrel didn't move. He was eating. The dove was larger than the squirrel and could have chased him away with a pecking. But the dove continued to walk the outskirts of the feeder, raising his wings and waiting for the squirrel to leave.

A small sparrow landed on the ground and hopped in to eat near the squirrel, finding tasty morsels. The dove continued to walk around the perimeter, raising its wings.

The tiny sparrow ate contentedly, and the small squirrel enjoyed a tasty meal. But the larger dove stayed on the periphery. He chose not to expand his perspective enough to see what he had.

> *"Where there is no struggle, there is no strength."*
>
> *Oprah Winfrey*

Are you like the dove? Do you wait until the food is convenient?

Are you willing to take risks like the sparrow? Can you eat with those who are bigger than you?

Are you like the squirrel? Do you hold your ground when intimidated by others?

Life is a process. Allow light and love to bless you as you find your way.

Chapter 38

A Higher Power

A higher power can be a healing influence in your life. I have found it to be so in mine. Most self-help programs recognize the influence of a higher power in the healing process. The human spirit seeks a higher power.

A young girl, Lyla, lived with foster care families. She was abandoned as a baby and had been brought up in "the system." The families she lived with over the years had no religion, so Lyla knew nothing about God or a higher power. She recalls that in her young life she needed someone or something to pray to, so she chose the sky. She would ask the sky to help her with her problems. The sky was someone she could talk to whenever she needed a listening ear. As she grew older, she found a religion that worked for her, but as a child she solved her problem in the best way she could—with the sky.

Find a higher power that works for you. Caring support of a group, organized religion, or the study of nature can connect you with the divine. Connect with a power greater than yourself in a way that will be significant to you.

Religious Ritual

Religion can bring ritual into your life, or you can create your own rituals, if you wish, according to your needs. As in all aspects of this book, you must write your own program. Make your own way. Find what will work for you.

Religion as a Healing Power

Positive energy will come to you as your affirmative thinking attracts it. Abuse survivors I worked with who believed in a higher power seemed to heal more completely than those who didn't.

Ciara survived brutal abuse as a child. As an adult she had become successful in her career, but haunting memories kept her stuck in depression. She struggled with difficult feelings as she retrieved the childhood recollections so she could discard them.

Through the healing process, Ciara relied on God and the curative power of her religious beliefs. While Ciara cleansed herself of old thinking patterns, she persistently looked to her God for help. Ciara believed her success in healing came from faith in God.

A higher power is a healing power.

Relationship with God

Why are people drawn to a relationship with God or a higher power? It has been so since the beginning of man. Erich Fromm, a Neo-Freudian psychoanalyst, believes that as humans we have anxiety at being separate from others. A relationship with God brings us to that place of belonging we all seek.

Best-selling author and spiritualist Tolle Eckhart believes Western cultures look at a love of God, in terms of belief in His existence, as a *thought* experience. Eastern cultures see the relationship with God as a powerful *feeling* experience, where one is inseparably attached to God and expresses her love for God in her daily acts of living.

These two cultural ideals culminate as one for me. Thinking and believing in God is a deep feeling experience which guides me to living daily acts of love so that I am accessing my divinity.

Think, Feel, Act

This type of living can only come through keeping thoughts, feelings, and actions focused on the divinity within you. Sometimes your center may slip and you may not stay as focused on this principle as you would like. But work to keep your daily focus.

Make religious study part of your life. You may become distracted by other things at times, but refocus yourself when that happens—be patient and persevere.

"God is, not was; He speaketh, not spake."
Ralph Waldo Emerson

Live your daily life as if you were one with God. Study wise teachers that lead you to the premise that

"There is but one good; that is God."
C.S. Lewis

Wise Teachers

There are many wise religious leaders who have walked the earth in the past. Choose to study one or many of the masters. There is not a right or wrong way. Find the way that will be best for you.

Read the works of these masters that bless mankind through their ideals of wisdom, love, and charity. Study them and you will access wisdom in yourself.

If you do not believe in a God or a wise teacher, find a higher power elsewhere. I had a couple of clients—survivors of incest—who could not stand to think of a man as a deity. They had not had good women in their lives either.

One of them used the rainbow as her higher power. It was a wonderful wise teacher for her, bringing her hope and brightness in the face of depression and despair. It helped her reframe her life in a positive way. She called upon the rainbow to help with her decisions, and her life gradually became a blend of beautiful colors.

Another client had a tall sturdy oak tree as her guide. It was strong and steady and an anchor for her inconsistent, flighty pattern of life. When she remembered to use the tree as her steadying influence, she did well.

Solitude as a Mentor

Sit under the stars for an evening. Watch the ducks float down a river. See the beauty in a growing plant. Walk with a child and watch him absorb the world.

> "Be still. Stillness reveals the secrets of eternity."
>
> Lao Tzu

Solitude can come in the quiet moments of your soul and speak to you as if you are one with God. Let it nourish you.

Let Yourself Be Guided

> "Let go and let God."
>
> Alcoholics Anonymous

This statement gives us the perspective that we are not in charge of the events of the world. Let yourself be guided. Let go and allow your higher power to bless you.

Allow divinity into your life in some way. It is healing and comforting.

> "No one saves us but ourselves. No one can and no one may. We ourselves must walk the path."
>
> Buddha

> "My religion is very simple. My religion is kindness."
>
> Dalai Lama

Chapter 39

Service

Gifts to yourself are gone when you are gone. Gifts to others live on as your legacy.

Service is one of the most powerful tools in the process of becoming whole. Give abundantly, and it will return a hundredfold.

> "One thing I know. The only ones among you who will be really happy are those who will have sought and found how to serve."
>
> Albert Schweitzer

I love service. I take pleasure in working with children, and I enjoy spending time with the elderly. Several days a week I assist older people in a church setting. These people are such an inspiration to me. They come in wheelchairs or with walkers or canes to give service themselves. Sometimes they are hard of hearing or can't see well, but they come. Their lives are rich and full because they give to others.

> "The best way to find yourself is to lose yourself in the service of others."
>
> Gandhi

Work with those around you to create something wonderful. Help in a soup kitchen for the homeless in your community. Spend time serving those who have suffered a disaster. Volunteer in the schools. Read to the elderly in a retirement community. Find some way to give back the abundance you have been blessed with.

> "It is high time that the idea of success be replaced by the idea of service."
>
> Albert Einstein

Find a humanitarian group that serves in third world countries or in poor areas around the world. Donate your time, expertise, or money to a project. The church I belong to asks youth to spend two years of their lives in service to others. When they return, they all say it was the best two years of their lives. Physicians take eyeglasses to Africa and perform dental surgery in Latin America. Humanitarians are in all areas of the world. I have a cousin who has just retired and is going to Africa to serve in the Peace Corps. She is very excited.

> "If we cultivate the habit of doing . . . service deliberately, our desire for service will steadily grow stronger and will make, not only our own happiness, but that of the world."
>
> Gandhi

Find a way to serve. Help a friend, listen to someone's problem, say hello to a neighbor, take in someone's paper, bake cookies for your dad, help out at a church, tell a teacher thank you after class, smile at someone. Serve your family, your friends, your church, your community, your nation, or the world. Serve the children of the world because they will lead us tomorrow. The gifts you receive back will be much greater than the small portion you give.

As you give abundantly, love will come back to you a hundredfold. The gifts you receive from service are much greater than the small gift given.

> "Goodwill to others is constructive thought. . . . The more such thought you attract to you, the more life you will have."
>
> Prentice Mulford

Chapter 40

Love

Love is the core of every good thing in life and the basis of every religion.

"Life in abundance comes only through great love."
Elbert Hubbard

What Is Love?

Webster's dictionary defines love as profoundly tender affection for others. Developing love takes humility, faith, discipline, and courage. Love is an attitude that comes from our thinking. We mistakenly think that we must find someone to love us, or we search for that perfect object—that beautiful woman or handsome man—to love. Many people call attraction love, but attraction is easy, fast, and it doesn't last. True love takes steadfastness and courage.

I know that in my own experience I wasn't loved until I learned to love. It wasn't about the other person in my life at all. It was about me learning the art of loving.

As I learn to love, I am loved.

Everyone is looking for the perfect mate with exactly the same interests, hobbies, religion, political stance, and cultural views. A garland of daisies is wonderful, but how much prettier is a bouquet that has a variety of flowers where we can appreciate each bloom for its uniqueness.

> "Love is that condition in which the happiness of another person is essential to your own."
>
> Robert A. Heinlein

A couple each lighted a candle as they began their wedding. They both held their lighted flame high until the culmination of the ceremony, where together they lit a single candle and blew their individual lights out.

What a sad symbol. We don't give up our individuality as we enter a relationship. Our uniqueness will aid us in nurturing a marriage to stand the tests of time. It will be built on the foundation of two separate entities coming together to create a family like no other. Our individualism will nurture the new bond of caring.

Each of us comes with our own personality. Granted, we all have to discipline and modify ourselves to live in the world. But can we also maintain our sense of self within the context of a love relationship? That's a task that I will work at the rest of my life.

Love of Family

As a child comes into a home, she needs to be loved. Parents can affirm the child's life and wants. Watching a child's personality develop is like seeing a beautiful rose open. We exclaim over each petal as it unfolds. A child establishes her view of herself as her self-concept develops. She sees herself as you see her—in the context of your vision.

> "Treat a man as he is and he will remain as he is. Treat a man as he can and should be, and he will become as he can and should be."
>
> Goethe

My grandmother planted a pear tree that produced the sweetest fruit. When I was a child, we used to climb up the branches to eat to our heart's content. The tree became old and woody and had to be cut down. So my mother planted another pear tree.

I grew up and married, and my children now love the pears from *their* grandmother's tree, just like I did when I was a girl. My mother dries the pears in her electric fruit dryer in the fall and sends little packages to her grandchildren, who live all over the country. They are grown now, with families of their own. The grandchildren keep the dried pears in the freezer and take one or two out for a snack when they want to be connected to their grandmother. Or they distribute the pears with their own children when sharing memories of her.

In our family, pears have come to mean love. Little acts of service connect us with each other. What does love mean in your family? What does your family stand for?

People who were adopted are often painfully aware of being disconnected. The clients I worked with solved this problem in various ways. One of them made an exhaustive search for her birth family. She found them and developed caring relationships with them. Another client surrounded herself with good friends that became her family. Another married someone who had a large, loving extended family and adopted them as her kin.

This past summer our family walked the paths that our ancestors trod on the Fox Islands off the coast of Maine. It was a life-changing experience for us. The family of the past became hauntingly real to us. I feel like I know those people. I am part of them, and they are part of me.

> *"Love is not primarily a relationship to a specific person; it is an attitude, an orientation of character, which determines the relatedness of a person to the world as a whole, not toward one object of love."*
>
> Erich Fromm

Brotherly Love

Do I care for those around me? Am I concerned about others? As I find myself in an attitude of love toward others, I can't help but feel that love for myself.

Gary Chapman, in his book *The 5 Languages of Love,* gives specific direction to our communication with others. As we use words of affirmation and empathize with others, we draw them close to us. Spending quality time with those around us and focusing on the daily happenings strengthens our relationships. Receiving gifts from others and performing acts of service increase love.

Are we not all connected as a human family? Each week I visit the sick in the hospital with a short message of comfort. Once, I saw a lady who had no family. A dear neighbor sat with her. The neighbor had found her friend collapsed on the kitchen floor and had taken her to the hospital. This small act of caring was not noted by anyone in this life but the two of them. No bells or whistles sounded. No speeches were made, but the world received the illumination of that love just the same. Each of them knew it because of the light they felt inside.

> "We cannot all do great things, but we can do small things with great love."
>
> Mother Teresa

Love Is an Attitude

Love is a thought defined by caring and kindness. Love must be practiced every day just as an artist practices the piano. Love takes patience to develop. One must overcome selfish tendencies and reach out to others. Love means to listen to others and be sensitive to their needs. Love is having faith in others and their gifts and goodness.

> "If you want to be loved, be lovable."
>
> Ovid

Love is the core of every good thing in life.

The butterfly is finally free from her chrysalis prison. She flies free to give and receive light, love, and beauty. These blessing come in copious numbers. She is richly blessed.

May you, like the butterfly, find beauty and blessings in life as you free yourself. Look for light and life—it is all around you, and it is yours.

You are free!

Conclusion

Monarch butterflies live as far north as Canada and migrate every year to Southern California and Mexico. They always know where to go. These delicate creations eat copious amounts of nectar to sustain them on their long flight and roost in trees along the way. Their life span allows them to make this journey only once, but they find their way with success and confidence.

As I study this alluring and seemingly fragile species, I realize they are anything but. Their work ethic is unsurpassed, for they traveling up to two thousand miles during their migration. Their self-care skills are admirable in that they make sure to drink plentiful amounts of nectar to sustain them throughout their journey. They avoid high winds and rain, which would damage their delicate bodies, and they stop to roost when they are tired. Their communication is unparalleled, for they have an innate ability to pass their expertise on to unborn generations of their magnificent species.

These lilting beauties set the standard for self-rec-reation high. I never pass one of these delightful creatures without contemplating their unrivaled example. They inspire me to become greater than I am, and to add beauty to the world in my small way. Follow them and their example as you journey toward Becoming Free.

Bibliography

Bandura, Albert. *Social Learning Theory*. Englewood Cliffs, NJ: Prentice Hall, 1976.

———. *Self-Efficacy in Changing Societies*. Cambridge, United Kingdom: Cambridge University Press, 1995.

Beattie, Melody. *The Language of Letting Go*. Hazelden, 1990.

Beck, Aaron. *Cognitive Therapy of Depression*. New York: Guilford Press, 1979.

Bernstein, Albert J. *Emotional Vampires: Dealing with People Who Drain You Dry*. New York: McGraw-Hill, 2002.

Bradshaw, John. *Bradshaw On: The Family, A New Way of Creating Solid Self-Esteem*. Deerfield Beach, FL: Health Communications, Inc., 1988.

———. *Creating Love: The Next Great Stage of Growth*. Westminster, MD: Bantam Books, 1992.

Burns, David. *Feeling Good: The New Mood Therapy*. New York: Harper Collins, 1999.

Byrne, Rhonda. *The Secret*. New York: Atria Books, Beyond Words Publishing, 2006.

Chapman, Gary. *The 5 Love Languages: The Secret to Love that Lasts*. Chicago, IL: Northfield Publishing, 1992.

Cleary, Thomas. *The Essential Confucius*. New York: Harper Collins, 1992.

Cline, Foster W. and Jim Fay. *Parenting with Love and Logic*. Bedford, OH: Pinion Press, 1990.

Cloud, Henry. *Integrity*. New York: Harper Collins, 2006.

Dass, Ram. *Journey of Awakening: A Meditator's Guidebook*. Westminster, MD: Bantam Books, 2004.

Eckhart, Meister, and Oliver Davies. *Selected Writings*. New York: Penguin Classics, 1994.

Emerson, Ralph Waldo. *The Essential Writings of Ralph Waldo Emerson.* New York: Modern Library, 2000.

Emmons, Robert A. *Thanks!: How the New Science of Gratitude Can Make You Happier.* New York: Houghton Mifflin, 2007.

Emmons, Robert A. and Michael E. McCullough. "Counting Blessings Versus Burdens: Experimental Studies of Gratitude and Subjective Well-Being in Daily Life." *Journal of Personality and Social Psychology* 84, no.2 (2003): 377–89. doi:10.1037/0022-3514.84.2.377.

Erikson, Erik H. *Childhood and Society.* New York: W. W. Norton & Company, Inc., 1950.

Fromm, Erich. *The Art of Loving.* New York: HarperCollins, 2006.

Gandhi, Mahatma. *The Words of Gandhi.* Edited by Richard Attenborough. New York: Newmarket Press, 2000.

Harbin, Thomas H. *Beyond Anger, a Guide for Men.* New York: Marlow and Company, 2000.

Harman, Amanda. *Butterflies (Nature's Children).* Danbury, CT: Grolier Educational, 1999.

Hemfelt, Robert, Frank Minirth, and Paul Meier. *Love is a Choice.* Nashville, TN: Thomas Nelson, 1989.

Hicks, Esther, and Jerry Hicks. *The Amazing Power of Deliberate Intent.* Carlsbad, CA: Hay House, Inc., 2006.

Knight, Rod. *Animals of the World: Monarchs and Other Butterflies.* Chicago, IL: World Book Inc., 2006.

Kornfield, Jack, *The Art of Forgiveness, Lovingkindness, and Peace.* New York: Bantam Books, 2002.

Margolis, Char and Victoria St. George. *Discover Your Inner Wisdom Using Intuition, Logic, and Common Sense to Make Your Best Choices.* New York: Simon & Schuster Inc., 2008.

Meyer, Laurine Morrison. *Sacred Home.* St. Paul, MN: Llewellyn Publications, 2004.

Miller, Gustavus Hindman. *10,000 Dreams Interpreted: A Dictionary of Dreams*. Edited by Hans Holzer. New York: Barnes and Noble Books, 1995.

Moore, Thomas. *Dark Nights of the Soul: A Guide to Finding your Way Through Life's Ordeals*. New York: Gotham Books, 2004.

No Cussing Club, last modified 2013, http://nocussing.com.

No Cussing Club, *YouTube*, last modified November 3, 2010, http://www.youtube.com/watch?v=IBCfXJBjVQg.

Norville, Deborah. *Thank You Power*. Nashville, TN: Thomas Nelson, 2007.

Phelan, Thomas W. *1-2-3 Magic: Effective Discipline for Children 2–12*. Glen Ellyn, IL: ParentMagic, Inc., 2004.

Potter, Ned. "'No-Cussing' Club Attracts Followers—and Thousands of Hate Messages." ABC News. Last modified January 16, 2009. http://abcnews.go.com/Technology/story?id=6665969#UZZqsaLvt8E.

Richardson, Cheryl. *The Unmistakable Touch of Grace*. New York: Free Press, 2005.

Sears, Martha, and William Sears. *The Discipline Book: How to Have a Better-Behaved Child*. New York: Little, Brown and Company, 1995.

Sumner, Holly. *The Meditation Source Book: Meditation for Mortals*. Los Angeles: Lowell House, 1999.

Thornton, Mark. *Meditation in a New York Minute: Super Calm for the Super Busy*. Boulder, CO: Sounds True, 2004.

Tolle, Eckhart. *A New Earth: Awakening to Your Life's Purpose*. New York: Penguin Books, 2006.

Vitale, Joe. *The Key: The Missing Secret for Attracting Anything You Want*. Hoboken, NJ: John Wiley and Sons, 2007.

Quotes

A Quotes. WordPress. Last modified 2013. http://www.aquotes.net/.

About.com. "Quotatons." About.com. Last modified 2013. http://quotations.about.com/.

Bartlett, John. *The Shakespeare Phrase Book Part One*. Cambridge, United Kingdom: University Press, 1880.

Benedict, Ruth. *The Chrysanthemum and the Sword: Patterns of Japanese Culture*. New York: Mariner Books, 2005.

Blue Health Advantage. "Preparing to Exercise." Wellness Councils of America. Last modified 2006. http://www.bluehealthadvantagene.com/individuals/health-library/brochures-and-guides/preparing-to-exercise/.

Brainy Quote. BookRags Media Network. Last modified 2013. http://www.brainyquote.com/.

Creativity for the Soul. "Gardens for the Soul & Design." Gardens for the Soul. Last modified 2006. http://www.creativityforthesoul.com/gardens.htm.

Das, Subharnoy. "Gandhi on God & Religion." About.com. Last modified 2013. http://hinduism.about.com/od/history/a/gandhiquotes.htm.

Denton, Bill. *CrossTies Devotionals*. Lulu Enterprises, Inc., 2003.

DragonflyAndromeda. "Follow your heart and your dreams will come true." deviantART. Last modified 2013. http://dragonflyandromeda.deviantart.com/art/Follow-your-heart-and-your-dreams-will-come-true-341793340.

Emmons, Robert A. *Gratitude Works!: A 21-Day Program for Creating Emotional Prosperity*. San Francisco: Jossey-Bass, 2013.

Feldman, Christina. *The Buddhist Path to Simplicity: Spiritual Practice in Everyday Life*. United Kingdom: HarperCollins, 2013.

Fisher, Mark. *The Instant Millionaire: A Tale of Wisdom and Wealth.* Novato, CA: New World Library, 1990.

Forgas, Joseph P., Joel Cooper, and William D. Crano., eds. *The Psychology of Attitudes and Attitude Change.* New York: Taylor & Francis Group, 2010.

Garner, Mary Cox. *The Hidden Souls of Words: Keys to Transformation through the Power of Words.* New York: SelectBooks, Inc., 2004.

Gibran, Kahlil. *Tears and Laughter.* Translated by Anthony Rizcallah Ferris. New York: Open Road Integrated, 2011.

Good Reads. Goodreads Inc. Last modified 2013. http://www.goodreads.com/.

Goodman, Joel. *Laffirmations: 1,001 Ways to Add Humor to Your Life and Work.* Saratoga Springs, NY: Health Communications, Inc., 1995.

Hill, Napoleon. *The Law of Success.* Mineola, NY: Courier Dover Publications, 2012.

Howard, Roland. "You Never Miss the Water, Till the Well Runs Dry." International Lyrics Playground. Last modified 2007. http://lyricsplayground.com/alpha/songs/y/younevermissthewater.shtml.

Hutchins, Paul. *The Secret Doorway: Beyond Imagination.* Cape Coral, FL: Imagination Publishing, 2009.

Internet Sacred Text Archive. John Bruno Hare. Last modified 2010. http://www.sacred-texts.com/tao/.

Jackson-Morris, Carla. *Just Hold On: Overcoming Private Emotions of Fear.* Xlibris Corporation, 2010.

Keen, Sam. The Board of Wisdom. Last modified 2013. http://boardofwisdom.com/togo/Quotes/ShowQuote?msgid=20/.

Kelly, Bob. *Worth Repeating: More Than 5,000 Classic and Contemporary Quotes.* Grand Rapids, MI: Kregal Publications, 2003.

Lincoln, Abraham. "About Lincoln." WordPress. Last modified 2013. http://abrahamlincolnthemovie.com/no-man-stands-so-tall-as-when-he-stoops-to-help-a-child-abraham-lincoln/.

Loewenberg, Lauri. *Dream on It: Unlock Your Dreams, Change Your Life.* New York: St. Martin's Press, 2011.

Markham, Dr. Laura. "It's Never Too Late to Have a Happy Childhood." *Aha! Parenting* (blog). Last modified 2013. http://www.ahaparenting.com/_blog/Parenting_Blog/post/It's_Never_Too_Late_to_Have_a_Happy_Childhood/.

Mieder, Wolfgang, Stewart A. Kingsbury, and Kelsie B. Harder, eds. *A Dictionary of American Proverbs.* New York: Oxford University Press, Inc., 1992.

Moore, Thomas. *Dark Nights of the Soul: A Guide to Finding Your Way Through Life's Ordeals.* New York: Penguin, 2004.

Muhammad. "The Infallibles." Al-Islam. Last modified 2013. http://www.al-islam.org/masoom/sayings/prophsayings.html.

———. "Quotations From The Prophet Muhammad." Yogananda. Last modified 2010. http://forum.yogananda.net/index.php?/topic/18467-quotations-from-the-prophet-muhammad-pbuh/.

Mulford, Prentice. *Kentucky New Era*, December 9, 2003. http://news.google.com/newspapers?nid=266&dat=20031125&id=KPYrAAAAI-BAJ&sjid=AG0FAAAAIBAJ&pg=5873,5268299.

Notable Quotes. Last modified 2013. http://www.notable-quotes.com/.

Public Quotes. Last modified 2013. http://publicquotes.com/.

Quotations Book. Last modified 2013. http://quotationsbook.com/.

Quotations Page, The. QuotationsPage.com and Michael Moncur. Last modified 2013. http://www.quotationspage.com/.

Quote Away. Last modified 2013. http://quoteaway.com/.

Reina, Dennis and Michelle Reina. *Rebuilding Trust in the Workplace: Seven Steps to Renew Confidence, Commitment, and Energy.* San Francisco: Berrett-Koehler, 2010.

Rowling, J. K. *Harry Potter and the Chamber of Secrets.* New York: Arthur A. Levine Books, 1999.

Search Quotes. Last modified 2013. http://www.searchquotes.com/.

Secret, The. Production Limited Liability Company. Last modified 2013. http://thesecret.tv/.

Sheep Dressed Like Wolves. Last modified 2013. http://www.sheepdressedlikewolves.com/theriots/.

Shelton, Charles M. *The Gratitude Factor: Enhancing Your Life Through Grateful Living*. Mahwah, NJ: Hidden Spring, 2010.

Shiromany, A. A., ed. *The Spirit of Tibet, Universal Heritage: Selected Speeches and Writings of HH The Dalai Lama XIV*. Bombay: Allied Publishers Limited, 1995.

Stanford. "Alfred North Whitehead." Stanford Encyclopedia of Philosophy. Last modified 2010. http://plato.stanford.edu/entries/whitehead/.

Think Exist. Last modified 2013. http://thinkexist.com/.

Wikipedia. "Serenity Prayer." Wikimedia Foundation, Inc. Last modified 3 May 2013. http://en.wikipedia.org/wiki/Serenity_Prayer.

Winfrey, Oprah. "Gratitude Elevates Your Life to a Higher Frequency." *Huffington Post*. November 22, 2012. http://www.huffingtonpost.com/oprah-winfrey/oprah-gratitude-thanksgiving_b_2171573.html.

Wisdom Fund, The. "Sayings: Learning—Prayer." The Wisdom Fund. Last modified 2013. http://www.twf.org/Sayings/Sayings4.html.

Witty Profiles. "Proverb Quote #6614362." Witty Profiles. Last modified 2013. http://www.wittyprofiles.com/q/6614362.

Ziglar, Zig. "A Quote by Zig Ziglar on Happiness, Journeys, and Success." Stream of Consciousness. Last modified 2013. http://blog.gaiam.com/quotes/authors/zig-ziglar/42119.

Zuck, Roy B. *The Speaker's Quote Book*. Grand Rapids, MI: Kregel Publications, 2009.

About Christy Monson

Christy Monson received a master's degree in Marriage and Family Therapy from UNLV and established a successful counseling practice in Nevada, counseling families and couples her entire career. She is the author of two young adult novels and one picture book, *Love, Hugs, and Hope: When Scary Things Happen*, a book helping young people cope with significant tragedy in their lives.

About Familius

Welcome to a place where mothers are celebrated, not compared. Where heart is at the center of our families, and family at the center of our homes. Where boo boos are still kissed, cake beaters are still licked, and mistakes are still okay. Welcome to a place where books—and family—are beautiful. Familius: a book publisher dedicated to helping families be happy.

Familius was founded in 2012 with the intent to align the founders' love of publishing and family with the digital publishing renaissance which occurred simultaneously with the Great Recession. The founders believe that the traditional family is the basic unit of society, and that a society is only as strong as the families that create it. Familius's mission is to help families be happy. We invite you to participate with us in strengthening your family by being part of the Familius family. Go to www.familius.com to subscribe and receive information about our books, articles, and videos.

Website: www.familius.com
Facebook: www.facebook.com/paterfamilius
Twitter: @familiustalk, @paterfamilius1
Pinterest: www.pinterest.com/familius